The
TOXIC PARENTS
Survival Guide

Recognizing, Understanding, and Freeing Yourself from These Difficult Relationships

Bryn Collins, MA, LP

Health Communications, Inc.
Deerfield Beach, Florida

www.hcibooks.com

Library of Congress Cataloging-in-Publication Data
is available through the Library of Congress

© 2018 Bryn Collins, MA, LP

ISBN-13: 978-07573-2104-7 (Paperback)
ISBN-10: 07573-2104-6 (Paperback)
ISBN-13: 978-07573-2120-7 (ePub)
ISBN-10: 07573-2120-8 (ePub)

Publisher: Health Communications, Inc.
        3201 S.W. 15th Street
        Deerfield Beach, FL 33442–8190

Cover design by Larissa Hise Henoch
Interior design and formatting by Lawna Patterson Oldfield

CONTENTS

PART THREE: **Making It Work**

Knowing others is intelligence;
knowing yourself is true wisdom.
Mastering others is strength;
mastering yourself is true power.

—Tao Te Ching

For Rod

Prologue

It's your first relationship and, when you're a baby, your most important one because it's how you stay alive.

Over your life, this relationship will have highs and lows. It will be among the most complex relationships you will ever have. In the great majority of cases, it will endure despite whatever happens. Like it or not.

For some lucky people, it will be a relationship filled with great rewards and much joy. For many people it will be a source of frustration, puzzlement, confusion, anger, attraction, and rejection interspersed with joy. And for some very unfortunate people, it's an unending nightmare or a vast frozen wasteland.

For those of you who fall among the lucky people, good for you! You won the lottery. Why are you reading this book?

For the many who spend a lot of time, energy, and often money to figure out this relationship, you have come to the right place. We're going to roll up our sleeves and figure this out together. We'll work toward positive management of these emotionally unavailable relationships as well as ways to feel better about yourself in the context of this primary relationship and the rest of the relationships in your life. Maybe you and your friends can find something else to talk about.

For the people who have endured nightmares or wastelands, we will explore some tools for you to use to break the chains that hold you stuck in the mess you didn't create but have had to live with. We will also talk about how to finally walk away from the toxic relationships once and for all.

We all have relationships with our parents. They are with us our entire lives, even after they no longer live. We need some different ways to deal with our parents' dysfunctions so that we don't suffer and don't pass along emotional unavailability to the next generation.

Just a quick note: The examples I use in the book are based on real cases or a compilation of real cases. Nobody's name is real, and details have been altered.

Introduction

Joyce's story:

The house phone was ringing as I came in the front door of my apartment, laden with my newly purchased second round of grad-school books that weighed a ton and had depleted my checkbook. I also had a bag with fresh fruit and veggies from the corner market and another from the fishmonger's shop across from my building.

I knew who was calling. I dumped my packages and snapped the lock on the door.

"Hi, Mom."

"So, what trouble did you get into today?" There was a note of humor that overlaid the usual accusation.

"I'm a grad student again," I responded, determined to ignore the bait.

"I suppose you need money. Again. You know, we're not made of money." This time the accusation was clear.

"No, I'm good. But thanks for the offer." We both knew it wasn't an offer, but I didn't want to escalate the situation by mentioning they hadn't paid for any of my education since undergrad fifteen years before.

"Are you sure this is what you want to do, this graduate school? You haven't done anything with your last two degrees."

I sighed. She apparently didn't need my help to escalate.

"Mom, I taught for two years after undergrad and . . ."

"And then you followed that man and wasted three years of your life." She had hated my boyfriend, particularly when we moved across country, and had chosen to ignore my several economic successes in those three "wasted" years, including a popular local television show on which she had been my guest several times.

I paused and took a deep breath. She didn't notice.

"And then you came back here and did nothing for another year." Again, choosing to ignore the successful small business I had started that continued to sustain my grad school habit.

"And then, of course, you couldn't just stay with us. You had to go running off to New York. Nice girls don't go to live by themselves in New York. Are you still thinking of being an actress, or was that just another failed flight of fancy?"

I took another deep breath. "Mom, I really don't want to get into this again. I've had a long day and I have some studying. . . ."

"Well, I suppose I shouldn't have any expectations." Big dramatic sigh. "After all, you've always been my problem child." That would be the kid with the 3.75 overall in high school and college who never missed a curfew or broke any rules. I was that problem child.

"You never could just do what other kids did. Look at Virginia. She has two beautiful kids, a darling husband, and a wonderful teaching job. She's done something with her life."

My blood pressure was rising and the temptation to lash out was almost overwhelming. In the back of my head I could hear my therapist's voice telling me not to feed into her conflict quest. I took another deep breath.

---

breathe . . . and don't engage!

"Mom, I've got a lot of reading to do and my groceries are getting warm."

"Okay, well, we love you and we miss you."

And that is a good example of an emotionally unavailable parent.

In this book we'll look at different types of emotionally unavailable parents, how emotional unavailability happens, how to manage the relationship and let yourself off the hook, and finally how to be an emotionally available parent.

PART ONE

What Is Emotional Unavailability?

1

Emotional Unavailability Defined

At its most basic, emotional unavailability is that feeling you have when someone holds you at arm's length and tells you it's your fault or smothers you out of your own life and experiences and then tells you it's not good enough.

Obviously, life isn't that simple, so let's break it down. People who are emotionally unavailable are unwilling or unable to invest emotions in a relationship. This takes many forms.

Sometimes emotional unavailability looks like busy-ness—someone in your life who just doesn't make space or time for you while reassuring you by telling you how important you are to them. They are always overcommitted and have an excuse for not interacting with you.

Sometimes it takes on the behavior of distance—the unmeltable iceberg. Other times emotional unavailability hides in secrets and lies. It can take the form of constant nagging or extreme hovering or smothering.

At its core, emotional unavailability is the inability of one person to connect with another in an emotional, appropriate way. Instead, the relationship is unstable, unmanageable, mysterious, and/or unfulfilling.

The reasons for emotional unavailability often come down to learned behavior in childhood or mental illness/personality disorders. People who are raised in a home or series of homes in which there is a disrupted emotional connection—or none at all—can carry that disruption into adult life and their own parenting style. Please note I said, "can." Not everyone who grows up in an emotionally disrupted system carries it forward. Many people whose childhoods were fire (abuse in all its horrible forms) or ice (negligence or stoic) have broken the patterns of the past and become wonderful, emotionally available, appropriate parents.

Mental illness has received a lot of attention recently but not always for the right reasons. Mental illness, like physical illness, occurs in a range of degrees from mild life disruptions to schizophrenia and everything in between. It can be one episode or a lifelong pattern. It can be mild and manageable or devastating and pervasive. No matter what form mental illness takes or how complicated or simple the treatment may be, mental illness has an impact on a family.

For example, perhaps the most common diagnoses of mental illness involve depression and anxiety. Unfortunately, these two diagnoses tend to run in families with both genetic and environmental underpinnings. I often hear clients say, "My family is so anxious. We are all worriers." Or they might observe, "Everyone in our family is depressed. We're all on medication." Mental illnesses such as depression, anxiety, bipolar disorder, or schizophrenia do have a genetic link, which, coupled with environment and experience, can show up throughout a family.

Personality disorders, on the other hand, are a pattern of behavior and personality quirks that have expanded and solidified to become an impediment to life functioning. While mental illness is often helped by medications coupled with therapy, personality disorders do not usually respond to medications, in general, and with some rare exceptions, don't change dramatically with therapy.

Anything that keeps people distant from their own feelings or those of others fits the definition of emotional unavailability.

In the following chapters, we explore many other examples of parental emotional unavailability in depth. Briefly, we'll talk about the following:

- **Inconsistent parents.** One day they're tyrants, the next they're almost indifferent. One day there are impossible rules; the next, no rules at all. We like people to be predictable. Parents who are not predictable create trust issues.

- **Just Not Good Enough.** No matter what you do, no matter how much you achieve, no matter how others honor and respect you, you will never be good enough to this parent. Expectations are a moving target. You get blamed for not reading their minds and living up to every moving target.

- **In His/Her Own Reality parents.** New World Order. Chemtrails. The Yeti. FEMA death camps. Martians making crop circles. The Zombie Apocalypse. Whatever they obsess about, it becomes their sole focus. It's not abusive or malicious but rather a distancing from life and reality—yours and the rest of the world's—and a distancing from relationships.

- **Hovering controllers** are parents who plan and watch everything their child does. These children grow up to be adults who know nothing about boundaries, making decisions, managing disappointment, or handling a crisis. Adult children of hovering controllers have to learn boundaries and be able to set them with parents who want nothing to do with boundaries and everything to do with your personal business.

- **Brainiacs are parents** who read all the books and blogs, listen to all the "experts," and follow every fad without thinking about the consequences to their kids. Their parenting is cerebral, and their kids are projects. As adults, the children of brainiacs have trouble trusting their own judgment and look to outside sources for wisdom and ignore their own good instincts.

- **Glory Days parents** are adults who desperately want not only to be friends with their kids but also their kids' peers. They might be in competition with their kids in sports, or for boyfriends or girlfriends, or dress in clothing appropriate for a much younger person. They might also compete intellectually or professionally or even with experiences. Their adult children need to learn about and set boundaries. They also need to learn how to disengage from the competition.

● **Blame Gamers.** It's your fault even if it isn't. The Blame Gamer is looking for someone other than her or himself to take responsibility for or accept the blame for any event in which they might look bad or be accountable. Parental Blame Gamers use their children as scapegoats. They have poor or non-existent boundaries. The consequences to the family are dissolution of trust and a weakening of bonds between parent and child.

● **Users and other emotional vampires** are parents who treat their adult children like a personal life bank. "Borrowing" money, cars, clothing, jewelry, and time with no effort to repay, appreciate, or restore is typical behavior. When, or if, confronted, they first make excuses, then become petulant or angry, accusing the adult child of betrayal. This behavior creates huge internal conflict for the adult child. We'll talk about ways to say no and not give in.

● **Mentally ill and personality disordered parents.** Mental illness affects not only the sufferer but also the families and children around them. Adult children of parents who are mentally ill have a lot of challenges. We'll talk in depth about diagnoses such as depression, anxiety, bipolar disorder (also known as manic depression), and schizophrenia. We'll also talk about personality disorders, those personality traits that are extremely maladaptive and ingrained, such as Borderline Personality Disorder, Histrionic Personality Disorder, Antisocial Personality Disorder, Passive Aggressive behavior, and Narcissistic Personality Disorder. We'll look at management tools and self-protection.

● **Addicted to _____.** Just as the adult children of persons who are mentally ill have major challenges dealing with the effects of the parents' behaviors, so also do those whose parents are or were addicted to alcohol or drugs, or habituated to shopping, lying, sex, or other behaviors and substances. We'll look at those effects and ways to overcome them.

- **Abusive parents.** Abuse takes a lot of forms—verbal, emotional, physical, sexual—none of them good. Adult children who have survived abuse can be angry or fragile. Sadly, they can also be abusers themselves. If you are a survivor of parental abuse, we will look at ways to move into healing and healthy patterns for yourself and your kids.

- **Absent parents.** Losing a parent to death, divorce, abandonment, or geography is hard, particularly if there is unfinished business or there are unanswered questions—or if the parents have used the child or adult child as a mediator or a messenger to an estranged parent. Finding ways to reconnect to resolve those incomplete relationships—with or without the absent parent—involves good boundaries and realistic expectations.

- **Toxic parents.** Sadly, some parents are not only incompetent or distant but genuinely toxic for their children by virtue of extreme abuse, extreme addictions, cults, extreme mental illness, or criminal behavior. For the adult children of toxic parents, we talk about closing that relationship safely and healing your heart.

- **Stepparents, grandparents, and in-laws.** These parental surrogates can either be great allies or great problems. They have the title but not necessarily the power, and sometimes their reach exceeds their grasp and they create issues within the family. Finding an appropriate way to help them define their role is extremely important.

Before we start, however, we need to cover some emotion basics so we're using a common language.

2

Emotion Basics

Like any skill, emotions have a language. Some people are lucky and learn it early. Other people, alternatively, get confusing or confounding teaching and just give up trying to figure out emotions and shut them off. Then there are people who are bombarded with so much emotional language they can't make sense of it because it's unconnected to their experience and just becomes word salad. Still others receive no emotional training at all and stay away from feelings their whole lives.

Learning how to feel and express your own emotions, interpret others' feelings, and mingle the two can start at any age, but the earlier, the easier. I've had a number of clients who were completely cut off from their feelings but, with persistence and education of how to connect with themselves and others, they have begun to recognize and act on feelings—their own and others. Emotions can be either simple and direct—mad, glad, sad, scared—or compound—combinations of the basic emotions.

Emotions have simple and compound names. Words like "confused," "frustrated," "amazed," "irritated," "mixed up," or "excited" are compound emotions and can mean several different things to both the speaker and the listener. Where people get in trouble is when those different things aren't clarified or expressed so that both conversants are operating from the same definition. For this reason, I always encourage people to use basic emotional words for clarity, particularly when talking about deep feelings or when just starting to practice expressing emotions clearly. You want to be sure both you and your conversant really know what you're trying to express.

Emotions are expressed internally and externally, physically and psychically. We've all had those moments when we felt one thing but our faces and bodies showed another:

"Do you want to hold my pet tarantula?"

"How do you like my special goat liver pate?"

"Does this dress make my butt look big?"

Your mouth might smile, but what you're feeling inside is another story, and your face will reveal that reality.

Body language—the physical expression of feelings—is a complex study, but in many ways we're all observers and interpreters, starting early in childhood, even before speech. It's how we read other people and determine if they're safe or dangerous, nice or scary, in agreement or opposed to what we're saying or doing. Body language is easily as complex as spoken language, yet even babies are experts in its interpretation.

Body language can be as obvious as a frown and crossed arms that say, "I am really mad and don't want to talk to you," or as subtle as the slight, skeptical lift of an eyebrow or a glance of the eyes. Researchers have studied subtle cues like eye movement and mouth position to connect body language with emotions. That field of research is called neurolinguistics and it's really revealing. We'll connect the internal feelings with external expression later.

But let's start with the basic building blocks of emotions. These four emotions are the foundation of most compound emotions:

Mad • Glad • Sad • Scared

If you want someone to really understand what you are feeling, use these "primary colors" when talking about your emotions. Compound emotional words might work with people who know you well, but don't leave anything to chance. Until there is completely clear feelings of communication between you, use the foundation emotions.

Let me give you an example. After we'd been married about three years, my husband and I had one of those married-people communication break-downs. We were working on installing a parquet floor—truly a fertile ground for misunderstandings in even the very best marriages. It wasn't going well.

Rod said, "I'm completely frustrated."

I said, "Me, too."

Wouldn't you think that was a clear communication of feelings? We'd both be wrong.

Rod began cleaning up and I was mystified.

To me, "frustrated" is a combination of *mad* and *scared*, as in, "I'm *mad* I can't figure this out and *scared* I won't be able to make it come together."

I said, "Help me understand why you're cleaning up."

He said, "I told you I was completely frustrated. That meant I was done with this. We have to hire a guy."

As we talked it out, we realized for Rod "frustrated" is *mad* and *sad*, as in, "I'm *mad* this doesn't work and I'm *sad* I can't make this come together, so I give up."

Hence, clearly communicating your emotions in basic terms has value. We understand one another very well—usually—but there's always room for improvement.

By the way, we hired a guy. And it took weeks to get all the random spots of glue completely off my body.

Help Me Understand: Magic Words

In my practice, I forbid couples to use the word "why" because why is always accompanied by the (sometimes) unspoken "the hell." It's an instant accusation whether you mean it to be or not.

If you need an explanation for something from your partner or your parent or your kid or your coworker or your boss (especially your boss), try using, "Help me understand. . . ." And don't follow it with "why."

"Help me understand your objectives."
"Help me understand your anger about this."
"Help me understand your objection to my idea."
And then listen closely and respectfully to the answer.
It is a fight stopper. You're asking for information, not accusing. It starts from the premise the other person had a valid reason for the choice they made and lets them know you are interested in their reasons for their decisions. Often you will find you have the same goals but different approaches. It's the opening of a respectful discussion in which both sides are ready to be heard.

Emotions are immediate, reactive, focused, and time limited. For example, we are sitting in my office talking. I change position in my chair and accidentally kick your shin very hard. You probably feel mad at me in *reaction* because you don't know if my behavior was intentional and you're not sure how to interpret it. You weren't mad before I kicked you, so it put you in the position of being immediately reactive to the event. Also you're not mad at anyone else; you're *focused* on me and my behavior. I quickly apologize profusely and offer to take you to the emergency room for which I will pay. You look at your shin and rub it a bit, but the pain is already fading and you accept my apology, *limiting the time* you are feeling mad. *Reactive, immediate, focused,* and *time limited.*

First let's take a look at each of the building blocks.

MAD

Think for a minute about the last time you were mad. Maybe during your commute or at your spouse or parent or boss or neighbor or that obnoxious commentator on the TV. Next, think about what that emotion felt like in your body as well as emotionally.

When you are mad, your body and your mind both participate:

● Your mind narrows your focus to a laser point on the subject of your anger. Some people talk about "seeing red" when they're really angry, which is an infusion of blood into your brain and eyes caused by a dilation of blood vessels to provide more nutrients to the brain and muscles of your arms and legs.

● Your body pumps adrenaline, a hormone produced in the adrenal glands situated atop the kidneys, one of the fight-or-flight hormones. Adrenaline, also called epinephrine, makes the heart beat faster to power the relocation of blood. It increases blood pressure by narrowing major blood vessels and sends a message to the brain: "Reroute blood to the arms and legs and get ready to fight or run." Adrenaline increases breathing and pulls blood away from the internal organs that are unneeded at the moment, like the stomach, liver, kidneys, and so on.

● Your fists clench; your voice gets louder; your face gets red; your body posture reflects the fight-or-flight message of adrenaline. You might pace or pound your fist on a table. You might even throw something or slam a door. People who cannot control their anger might become physically violent or murderous.

Mad is a powerful emotion. If it's overused or the only emotion someone ever seems to feel, it becomes much less powerful but more debilitating. People around a chronically mad person come to expect them to respond to any and all situations with anger, so dismiss it as just more of the same. Meanwhile, the mad person finds himself or herself not feeling heard or respected and is not getting the response he or she hoped for, so the situation escalates, which can be physically and emotionally harmful.

SAD

Just as we did with mad, now remember the last time you felt sad and think about what that felt like in your body and your emotions. Sadness is both mentally and physically oppressive, expressed in body and brain. Your body reflects your brain chemistry. People who are sad seem to compress in on themselves: their shoulders slump; their chests cave in; their heads droop; they keep their arms close to their bodies. Their faces lack sparkle and smiles are gone. Their eyes look down.

Your brain, in a complex chemical/electrical dance, makes seventeen different chemicals called neurotransmitters, which neurons—the nerve cells—use to transmit messages from one to another. If the process were all electrical, thought wouldn't be possible because the information flowing into the brain from your body would be moving too fast to capture. If it were all chemical, it would be too slow. The combination is, in the words of Goldilocks, "just right!"

Several of those neurotransmitters affect mood. Maybe you've heard of serotonin as the "happiness controller." If our serotonin isn't concentrated enough or doesn't stick around long enough between neurons, our moods get low. Too much serotonin doesn't mean you're excessively happy. In fact, it's dangerous, bringing on "serotonin syndrome," in which the person may feel agitated and experience rapid heart rate, stomach disruptions, shivering, or muscle rigidity. In severe cases, serotonin syndrome can cause seizures, high temperature, irregular heartbeat, and unconsciousness. Emergency medical intervention would be critical. With all neurotransmitters, the Goldilocks principle prevails. There is a "just right" zone.

Another mood neurotransmitter is norepinephrine. *Nor* is Greek for "just like," and epinephrine is another name for adrenaline. So norepinephrine acts in the brain in the same way epinephrine/adrenaline behaves in the body: It's an internal stimulant. Too little or too weak norepinephrine and you have low energy. Too much norepinephrine and you become manic.

Too little norepinephrine and too little serotonin, and you have a low mood with little energy. That sounds a lot like how sadness feels. It's also what contributes to depression. Sadness is the emotion. When sadness goes on too long, it can become depression.

SCARED

Most people have felt scared at one time or another, sometimes as a part of something fun or exciting like a roller coaster or a horror movie and sometimes something much more serious like a car accident, war, or a missing child or parent. As we did with mad and sad, take a minute to remember a situation in which you felt scared and reflect on how that felt in your emotions and your body. Scared and mad share the adrenaline/ norepinephrine rush and the accompanying fight-or-flight energy. The differences, however, are important.

Scared is more aimed at flight than fight. Although the body is prepared for both, common sense and biology make us more prone to leaving a scary situation. The blood still moves to the limbs and the brain, but rather than the narrow focus of mad, the brain begins assembling details of the situation and becomes superattentive to the environment, called hyper-vigilance, gathering information not only for the present but to store and function as a "remember this" warning system for future similar situations.

On a roller coaster, scared emerges as a scream of part joy, part excitement, and part fear. At a horror movie, you gasp and huddle with your friends, giggling at your fears but feeling your heart race. A little scared can be fun.

But if your car is skidding out of control on black ice or someone is shooting at you or your four-year-old has wandered off or a bunch of other terrible things are happening, your body and brain are flooded with awareness and you begin observing and gathering information instantly. Your brain stores the cross-references under the categories of all the senses while making split-second decisions about how to escape, be safe, and solve problems.

Much of what scares us is transitional. You figure out where that strange noise is coming from in the middle of the night and realize it's a tree branch scraping on the window, then kind of chide yourself for being scared and go back to sleep. Your four-year-old emerges from his hiding place, laughing that he was able to fool you. You regain control of your car and pull over to the side of the road to catch your breath. Your heart pounds for a few minutes more as your body processes the remaining adrenaline, but soon your heart and breathing return to normal and you go back to what you were doing before the scare.

When what scares you occurs repeatedly or nearly takes your life or the life of someone you love or even a stranger, your brain uses flashbacks and nightmares to remind you of what happened, particularly if you are in the same area or other things like sounds or smells trigger the memory warning system. When we lived in the caves, those alarms protected the people who were good at responding to them so that they could make more people. We are the long-distant children of those who possessed sharpened senses. Those reissued warnings in the absence of immediate danger are symptoms of posttraumatic stress disorder (PTSD; now being referred to as posttraumatic stress syndrome [PTSS]), one of the anxiety disorders.

Sometimes people who are scared look like they're mad. Think of the humble puffer fish. They are physically adapted to how they live: on the reef, eating little reef critters. Their bodies are boxy and their fins are small, meant more to stabilize them in the water than to move rapidly or efficiently. When they feel threatened, they fill with water and the spikes that lie flat when they're calm suddenly pop up. Their message is "If you bite me, I will hurt you." The same principle applies to people who are scared. They feel threatened, so they puff up and get aggressive. They appear to be mad, but underneath the bluster hides scared. The message is still "Don't hurt me."

Scared is not a bad thing. It keeps us aware of our surroundings and attentive to what we're doing. Like everything else, too much scared isn't good for the mind or body. Too little scared might put you in unsafe situations. It's Goldilocks again: seeking the just right.

GLAD

This one requires the least explanation: The emotion of joy is exquisite—a reflection of a life and mood in perfect balance. Your body and mind are in sync; you smile with your mouth, your eyes, and your body.

The one glitch with gladness is for people who are anxious or have PTSD/PTSS. Excitement can feel a lot like fear. Its body effects can be very similar. If you are an anxious person, be aware that a good thing can feel scary. Pay attention to the context.

SO WHAT?

Most everyone feels the basic four emotions whether they are able to identify them. Emotions by themselves are neither good nor bad. They're simply feelings. What we do with those feelings and how we talk about them are what gives them meaning.

When you're dealing with people who are unconnected with what they feel but they're still feeling it and just don't know how to identify what they're experiencing, you have to use basic language about emotions to get them to talk in feelings language and begin to connect with their emotions. Start with the building blocks—and sometimes staying with the basics is your best bet.

MINDSETS

Remember earlier in this chapter when I talked about emotions being immediate, reactive, focused, and time limited? Those are the qualities of the basic four emotions and also of compound emotions.

When a person gets stuck in one emotion that's used all the time as the first response to any situation, that emotion has become a mindset. Mindsets are *pervasive, responsive, generalized,* and *long-lasting.* They are the first and sometimes the only emotion a person uses or feels in any situation. Each of the basic four emotions has a corresponding mindset.

Pervasive means that mindset dominates the way a person looks at the world. *Responsive* means the mindset is the person's consistent response to every situation. *Generalized* means the person lumps all vaguely similar situations into one general bucket and then responds pervasively to all those situations. Mindsets are *long-lasting*—often lifelong—and form the core of a person's responses to most of the world.

For example, a person whose mindset is anxious sees the vast majority of others in the world as a threat even though those people may never have made any sort of threat against them. It is their pervasive, generalized response.

Jerry was scared of groups of people because once when he was in Chicago he had been pushed around, threatened, and robbed by a group of teenage boys. His fears had morphed into anxiety, and he became fearful of any group of people, even elders, in a change called generalizing. He simply couldn't tolerate being around crowds because he would have terrible anxiety attacks. Anxiety became his mindset. We were able to use exposure therapy to help him conquer his fears and lower his anxiety level. We did a lot of mall walking through crowds.

---

mindset Angry ➤ emotion Mad
mindset Glad ➤ emotion Joyful
mindset Scared ➤ emotion Anxious
mindset Sad ➤ emotion Regretful

Angry

The angry mindset person chooses mad as the primary feeling response to all emotional situations. The person might then move on to another emotion basic, but the first stop is always mad. Their signature phrase is, "Yes, but ..."

Let's say an angry mindset person wins the lottery. "Why would that person be mad?" you might ask, but if you think about it, the first emotional stop of mad could be, "*Yes,* I won *but* now I have to deal with all the greedy friends and relatives I haven't heard from in years." Or "It's probably all gonna get sucked up by taxes." After that initial mad response, the person might move on to feeling glad, but mad is almost always the first stop.

Joyful

And then there are the joyful people. They go through life seeing sunshine and flowers, looking for and finding the best in every day. The only problem for joyful mindset people is they are not always good at seeing trouble coming toward them. Unlike anxious people who overpredict bad things or regretful people who try to fix things that have already occurred or angry people who burn the house down with a flamethrower just to get rid of a spider, the joyful person lives in a blissful present, untroubled by possibilities. Their catchphrase is, "Don't worry about it."

The only problem for joyful people is they are sometimes very bad at predicting outcomes. Their laissez-faire attitude makes them vulnerable to surprising bad events because they have not rehearsed the possible negatives in their minds.

Anxious

The anxious mindset person's first stop is scared. Their catchphrase is, "What if . . . ?" and that question usually sets off speculation about a future filled with scary possibilities. The following story appeared in the *Minneapolis Star Tribune*, and I remember giggling about it at the time. I'm paraphrasing the story. It's the perfect tale to illustrate the anxious mindset.

A number of years ago a man who lived in Fargo, North Dakota, had bought a Powerball ticket in Minnesota because North Dakota didn't participate in the lottery. He stuck it on the door of the fridge with a magnet, and miracle of miracles, he matched all the numbers and won. I knew immediately on reading the article he was an anxious mindset person because rather than just putting the ticket in a safe place until he could make the trip down to St. Paul to the Minnesota lottery office to collect his winnings, he called an armored truck company and had them park the truck with two armed guards in his driveway to keep the ticket safely guarded until the following Monday when he and his wife piled into the armored truck along with the guards and made the three-plus-hour drive to the Twin Cities. Obviously, his initial response to the win was scared.

When you let anxiety do your thinking, you might not make the best decisions. Nobody had known he had the winning ticket but once the truck showed up in his driveway, people got very curious and everybody knew, putting the guards and the ticket at much more risk—not to mention the discomfort of riding in an armored truck for seven hours round-trip.

Regretful

The regretful mindset person's first stop is sad. Regretful people live in the past and mourn their inability to change it. Their key phrase is usually,

"If only." Using the lottery win example again, the regretful person might sigh deeply, then say, "Oh, if only this had happened twenty years ago when I really needed the money," or "if only I didn't have to have my name in the paper. I just know I'll be deluged with calls and I don't like to talk on the phone." Again, the person may move on to feeling another emotion, but the first stop is almost always going to be sad.

 ## What Is Your Mindset?

Read each of the following scenarios and choose the answer that most clearly fits your reaction. Be honest—you're the only person you have to share this with.

A   B   C   D

1. If I'm stuck in traffic, I'm most likely to
    A. Drum my fingers on the wheel and worry about being late
    B. Brood about my rotten luck
    C. Get up really close to the car in front of me and blow my horn
    D. Listen to the radio

2. If a cashier shortchanges me, I
    A. Worry the manager won't believe me if I complain
    B. Just accept it as typical of my luck
    C. Slam my fist on the counter and demand to see the manager
    D. Mention it to the cashier

3. If the TV remote stops working, I
    A. Get very flustered and assume I've broken it
    B. Think it's just one more thing going wrong
    C. Throw it at the TV
    D. Check the batteries and replace them and/or read the manual

4. If someone is sitting in the seat I have tickets for at an event, I

    A. Worry about confronting the person because he or she might be violent

    B. Assume my tickets are invalid

    C. Get a cop to throw the bum out

    D. Ask the person to check his or her seat number

5. If my child gets a D in algebra, I

    A. Lie awake worrying she won't get into college and will have to work at low-paying jobs without opportunity all her life

    B. Remember how bad my grades were in high school

    C. Ground her for the rest of high school

    D. Offer to help or get a tutor and, if she chooses neither, let it go with words of encouragement, support, and empathy; she has to learn how to work through life problems, and we're there if she needs us

6. If a neighbor's stereo is too loud and I can't sleep, I

    A. Lie awake and try to decide how to ask them to turn it down without making them mad

    B. Lie awake and think about my rotten luck to live next to this fool

    C. Pound on my neighbor's door and threaten violence

    D. Phone and politely ask the neighbor to turn it down

7. I believe the lottery is

    A. A possible way to solve all my financial worries forever

    B. Rigged

    C. Always won by some jerk who never bought a ticket before

    D. Fun to dream about what I would do with so much money

8. If my neighbor borrows my lawn mower, I

    A. Worry his kids might get hurt by it and I will end up getting sued and losing everything

    B. Assume they'll either never return it or return it broken

    C. Track them down to make sure I get it back right on time

    D. Am glad to loan it to them to help them out and have the bonus of getting to see them and get caught up

9. I have a strange pain in my back so I

    A. Agonize about making a doctor's appointment, then worry it's cancer and I'm going to die
    B. Assume it's cancer and I'm going to die (Who can afford doctors?)
    C. Feel really put out I have to take time off from work (Why aren't doctors in their offices when real, working people don't have to miss work and risk getting fired?)
    D. Make a convenient appointment and have it checked out

10. My spouse is late coming home from work, I

    A. Assume he or she has been in an accident and is bleeding to death in a ditch somewhere; I decide what time I'll start calling emergency rooms. then watch the clock
    B. Assume he or she is up to something
    C. Am really mad and blow up his or her phone with texts and messages
    D. Am happy to see him or her when they arrive at home and tell me about their day

11. I get a speeding ticket so I

    A. Wonder how long it'll be before my insurance rates go up and I have to get a second job to pay for car insurance
    B. Assume the cop had been hiding there waiting for me
    C. Go ballistic and tear it up where the cop can see me
    D. Pay it and remind myself to ease up on the lead foot

Now look back at the scoring grid and see where most of your marks are clustered. If the majority are in the A group, you have a primarily anxious mindset. The largest concentration in the B section indicates you have a regretful view of the world. A cluster of the most marks in the C area reveals an angry mindset. If the majority are D answers, you are a joyful person.

It would be rare to find all the marks in one area. However, if you find a large cluster in one zone, you will want to do some work in that part of your life. If the distribution is about even among three or four areas, you are a person of many facets but not a dominant mindset. That actually shows balance and self-awareness as well as adaptability and the ability to respond to a situation rather than react. These are all good things, for sure.

Remember, your mindset is how you look at the world. It's your base of emotional operations and probably has been for a long time. It's not easy to change your mindset, but if you want to, you can begin by catching yourself reacting to the situations you encounter in daily life. Ask yourself, *Am I reacting or responding? How do I really feel? Is my response appropriate and proportional to the situation?* At first it will be a daunting task to try to catch yourself and ask the questions, but the more you do, the less time it will take. You can go back and take the quiz again later to see your progress and celebrate your change.

Once you know your own mindset—and we all have one to a lesser or greater degree—you can do a couple of things. First, you can work on experiencing and expressing a broader range of the basic four emotions—mad, glad, sad, scared—staying in touch with the immediate reaction that's appropriate to the situation rather than jumping to your default position.

People with Good Boundaries . . .

✓ Are assertive, not aggressive

✓ Stay in a Solver spot (We come to that in the next chapter.)

✓ Use clear communication

✓ Are in touch with their feelings

✓ Keep private information private

✓ Neither give nor receive inappropriate gifts, sex, or contact

✓ Are clear in their various roles in life

✓ Don't use sex as a substitute for love

✓ Don't give gifts to get favors or advantages

✓ Are respectful of other's bodies, turf, thoughts, and feelings

✓ Don't tell everything

✓ Don't gossip

✓ Have clear, readable emotions

✓ Are able to identify bad boundaries in others

✓ Don't automatically expect others to fill their needs

✓ Don't believe others can or should be able to read
  their minds

✓ Don't permit self-abuse, sexual abuse, physical abuse, verbal
  abuse, or emotional abuse by another for any reason

✓ Don't allow others to define them or their reality

✓ Don't allow others to take or give without limits

Second, you can identify others' mindsets and use that knowledge to better approach them in an emotional situation. This helps you stay in control and seek a solution to a problem rather than looking for someone to blame or hold responsible, which leads to much better relationships.

And you need to set boundaries.

BOUNDARIES

Boundaries are, in essence, knowing where you begin and someone else ends. People with poor boundaries want to be in the middle of your life, where they don't really belong. People with good boundaries know when to stop. They wait for you to ask for their help or input. They show you physical and emotional respect. They ask what you need instead of assuming they know better than you what you might require.

People who have poor boundaries ooze all over your life without a bit of remorse or even awareness they're doing anything wrong. They don't take into account what your obligations or plans might be, just what they want. They will show up unannounced and expect you to drop everything and tend to them. They will make commitments that include you without talking to you first. They'll come to visit and rearrange your kitchen. They'll tell you how to handle your money or raise your kids or what you "should" be doing without acknowledgment that you are able—and willing—to make your own decisions.

Remember, "No" is a complete sentence
that creates good boundaries.

When you're dealing with a parent—or anyone for that matter—who has poor or no boundaries, you are left with the responsibility to set boundaries. You do that by politely saying, "No, thanks," when intrusive advice is given; by saying, "I wish I had the time to visit right now, but I'm in the middle of something," or by saying, "I have other plans that day. I wish you'd checked with me first." In other words, you are entitled to make your own choices and live your life as you choose, without unsolicited input or demands.

3

Emotional Dynamics

There are other facets of emotions we need to cover before we look at our difficult or downright dysfunctional parents. We'll look at trust and the critical role trust plays in our relationships with others and with ourselves. We will then use our learning about the elements of trust to explore the five spots of Emotional Location. This tool can help you not only to see where others may be coming from in an emotional situation but also to help you choose where you want to be in the situation rather than reacting from a dysfunctional place. We will also look at communication skills and using emotional language to create trust and communication.

TRUST

I can't overstate the role trust plays in emotions and relationships. Trust is the foundation upon which we build emotional intimacy. Trust in a relationship provides safety for the participants. Knowing we can trust people's words, intents, and actions smooths the way for people to open their hearts.

Conversely, breaches of trust build a foundation of doubts and lies that crumbles easily and destroys relationships.

With parents and kids, trust is an essential part of the relationship from the very beginning. The baby has to trust the parents to provide safety and food—basic life needs. Adolescents might test the trust in the relationship: lying about friends, whereabouts, grades, homework, drugs, alcohol, or sexual activities. It's part of the development of adolescents. Come on—as adults, when we're with our friends, we all have those stories about rotten choices in our teens and twenties and we tell them with a mixture of fondness and relief we survived our era of stupidity. Adolescents and twenty-somethings need to make bad choices to learn why they're called bad choices.

Good judgment comes from experience.
Experience comes from bad judgment!

Parents, on the other hand, must not break trust with their kids. If parents catch their kids lying, there must be consequences appropriate to the magnitude of the lie or bad action. Parents cannot lie to their kids, abandon them, use drugs, be alcoholic, be abusive, or be promiscuous without breaking the essential bond of trust.

FOUR ELEMENTS OF TRUST

Trust is made up of four elements. These elements working together— trust, Emotional Location, communication and emotional language—create deep and authentic connections between people and are the foundation of real connection. Take away one of them, and trust is broken. Once trust is broken it needs to be rebuilt. Think of it as a trust account at the First National Bank of You: If you overdraw your trust account, either at the bank or in your relationships, you must make deposits to build that account back up. We'll talk more about that after we look at the four elements.

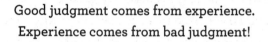

Predictability ➤ Reliability ➤
Truthfulness ➤ Honesty

Predictability

Sometimes you hear people imply predictability is a bad thing. "She's so predictable, she always has the same lunch every day."

In terms of trust, predictable is a good thing. It means you are today who you were yesterday and who you will be tomorrow. It means you can be counted on.

People who are unpredictable create trust issues. If someone tells you he will meet you at your favorite restaurant at 5 PM on Tuesday and he doesn't show up, you call him. If his excuse isn't plausible or an explanation or apology isn't even attempted, you might still be friends, but your trust will be injured if not broken and he will need to make some deposits in the trust account.

How does a person make deposits in the trust account? By being predictable, reliable, truthful, and honest over a long period of time. Everyone makes mistakes. An apology, a reasonable explanation or excuse, and returning to the basic trust elements goes a long way. If, however, the mistake is repeated or the explanation doesn't make sense or there is no apology or attempt to change behavior, trust is eroded. By making a sincere apology for a transgression of trust, by not repeating the error, by returning to demonstrating trustworthiness, deposits accrue. It's a great idea to always be in the black in your trust account with loved ones.

Reliability

Reliability means that your word is your bond. If you agree to take care of something, it will be done on time and correctly. A person's troubles might start with an abundance of reliability in a family of unpredictable, unreliable people. If you are the only one in the family who is reliable, your trust is repeatedly broken. Beyond such a breach, people look at your family and assume you are like them, no matter what you do. You end up being the one who takes on the responsibility for the whole family's behavior. You can see how unreliable behavior has negative effects on a family because trust gets repeatedly broken. Children from such a family grow up not trusting others. Broken trust breaks families generation after generation.

People who are reliable are consistent across time. You know when they tell you something it will be true and it will occur as they say it will. Children of reliable parents generally grow up to be trusting and reliable themselves.

Truthfulness

Truthfulness is the accurate reporting of verifiable fact. If I tell you it's seventy-two degrees outside, you can look at your cell phone weather app or a thermometer and verify I'm accurately reporting the fact. Conversely, if I tell you it's seventy-two outside and you look out the window at a roaring blizzard, my truthfulness is highly suspect and I'm breaking trust.

In a family relationship, accurate reporting of verifiable facts is critical. Without accurate information and consistent truth telling, more broken trust arises.

Honesty

Honesty is accurately reporting feelings. If you've been dating someone for a week and she tells you she loves you, that's very probably more manipulation than honesty. Trust comes before love. People who understand and know their feelings are honest about them and expect honesty in return. People who get stuck in a particular mindset have difficulty expressing emotions honestly because of their default to the associated emotion that makes them hard to read and hard to trust.

REPAIRING TRUST

Remember the trust account idea? Making deposits in the trust account is a daily responsibility in a healthy relationship. Your relationship trust account should always be in the black. Way in the black.

So how to do that? That's easy: be predictable, reliable, truthful, and honest. And if you slip, own it immediately, make a sincere apology, and then endeavor not to make the same mistake again.

Everybody makes mistakes in relationships. It's what you do to repair the mistakes that builds trust.

If you're on the receiving end of trust busting, you have the right to ask for an apology—a sincere apology—and to clearly name the violation. If you're dealing with a parent who has broken your trust repeatedly, you have the right to identify the violations and the consequences those violations have caused for you.

Making an Apology

A sincere apology is not just a quick "Sorry."

Instead, a sincere apology has three steps:

1. Looking the offended person in the eyes and saying sincerely, "I'm sorry I didn't pick you up at your meeting as I said I would. I'm really embarrassed." In that way you not only apologize but you also own your behavior in a very clear way.
2. An offer of restitution: "I know you had to take a cab when I didn't pick you up. May I pay for your cab fare?"
3. A guarantee of no repetition: "Next time I offer to pick you up, you can count on me being there."
   Then be there.

USING "I FEEL" LANGUAGE

Now you're familiar with the four basic emotions—mad, glad, sad, and scared—and their associated mindsets and you understand how important it is to communicate emotions clearly. "I feel" language is a very useful tool to communicate with anyone, emotionally available or not. It's also called "reflective listening."

Here's the basic form to follow:

You: "Dad [or Mom or their name], I feel scared when you encourage my kids to ride roller coasters."

Dad: "Son [or Daughter or other], I hear you say you feel scared when I encourage your kids to ride roller coasters. Help me understand what scares you."

You: "Dad [or other], I am scared of riding roller coasters, and when you talk to the kids about them you make them sound really fun and exciting. I get scared something might happen to you or one of the kids. Especially those really fast ones that go upside down."

Dad: "Son [or other], there are many people who safely ride roller coasters every day. If it would help, I can look up the statistics for exact numbers of injuries, but I assure you the number is very small. However, I would never want to disrespect your concerns for your children, so would you prefer I didn't talk about coasters at all or is there a compromise?"

You: "Dad [or other], I don't want my kids to grow up being fearful of experiences, and I suspect if they have a mild, kid-appropriate roller-coaster experience this summer, it would be okay. Maybe if you'd take them to somewhere safe—like not a carnival but a real amusement park with permanent rides and a real maintenance crew—and ride the kid coaster with them, that would be a place to begin. But please don't encourage them yet to ride the really scary ones."

So this is an ideal "I feel" language example in which both parties know the form, use the three-sentence rule I discuss later, stick to the subject, and look for an equitable solution.

THE FORM

Ideally, we would teach our kids to communicate this way from the first time they can string a sentence together. Unfortunately, that rarely happens. The good news is that reflective listening / "I feel" language can be learned and can become a habit. At first it's awkward because it's a new skill and takes concentration. The more you use it, the more natural it feels, and the more natural it feels, the more comfortable it becomes. Let's break this down.

First, the initial sentence. You notice every exchange begins with a name or title. People listen more closely when you begin a sentence with their name or title, and the objective of this tool is to be sure your feelings are heard correctly and clearly.

Also keep that sentence short and to the point. Begin with "I feel" and then say the name of the feeling using one of the basic four. Next say what elicits that feeling. You are setting the parameters for the conversation and establishing the subject. Then stop and let the other person or second party speak.

The response. Again, second party, begin with a name or title. It shows respect. Then say, "I hear you say," and repeat precisely what you just heard the first party say. Don't paraphrase because it sounds like you didn't really listen. Then ask for clarification. "Help me understand" is a really good phrase to use. Conversely, "why" is not because "why" sounds accusatory or is followed by the unspoken "the heck" (or worse). Then stop speaking and let the first party answer.

The explanation. First party, this is your opportunity to explain your feelings. This is where the three-sentence rule kicks in. Keep it simple but clear. In the example above, the first party explains the fear and creates a context for the feelings. You notice there is no accusation and no pointing fingers. Don't say anything like, "You made me scared of roller coasters when I was a kid so I don't want you to scare my kids." That's a conversational shutdown and a change of subject. It's also accusatory. People tend not to cooperate with others who accuse them of something they didn't intend to do.

The discussion and solution. Sticking to the subject and staying with the three-sentence rule, this is the time to look for a solution that feels fair to both parties. Notice in the example above that both parties are looking for a compromise. Obviously, some topics require a solution, not a compromise, such as having to set firm boundaries or confronting inappropriate behavior. Then you have to be firm and stand your ground.

"No, you cannot take my five- and six-year-old kids on the 'most dangerous coaster in the world.'"

THE SUBJECT

Critical to the whole process is that you stick to one subject. Most people go off the rails in emotional conversations when they throw everything into the bucket. You can only solve one problem at a time, so only present one problem at a time for solution. In the example, the first party could have messed up the opportunity for solving the problem by adding blame for the fears of roller coasters. The second party could have become defensive or angry and derailed the process.

The first speaker's responsibility is to establish the subject of the discussion. The second party's responsibility is to listen respectfully, respond appropriately, and stick to the subject.

THE SOLUTION

Ideally, the conversations flow like the example and everyone looks for a solution. People and families who practice and use "I feel" language and commit to using the technique make it work. *Practice* is the important word here. It takes practice, focus, and commitment by both parties to using "I feel" language, sticking to the subject, and finding a solution.

What to do when it goes awry? Let's assume you are the first party and have practiced so that you are a master at "I feel" language and are seeking a solution. Instead of listening and responding using the technique, the second party gets mad or defensive or attacks. Because you are a master, you know to repeat your first statement and then add, "I hope we can discuss this and find a solution." Stick to your point and your subject. You may have to do it again, at which time you can add, "Can you please repeat what you heard me say? It will help us find a solution."

It takes a lot of practice to remember to use "I feel" language in emotionally charged situations, and even masters of the technique sometimes fail at it. The trick is to practice it, teach it to your kids and parents—and spouses, friends, and coworkers for that matter, and try to make it an active part of your tool kit.

Speaking of solutions, next we're going to talk about how people can become solution focused, why they don't, and how you can help yourself and others achieve solution nirvana.

EMOTIONAL LOCATION

Now we've considered emotions, mindsets, and the elements that contribute to emotions, like trust, boundaries, and communication skills and some tools to go with each. Using the tools helps us to be emotionally available to our partners, parents, children, friends, and coworkers. Good tools also help us manage people who don't choose to change.

Ultimately, change is a matter of choice. The only person who can make the decision to change is that person. You can't force or wish or manipulate someone into making the decision to change. It has to happen from the inside out. No matter how much you'd like your parents or your kids to change, it is impossible for you to force change to occur. Remember, people only change when they become too uncomfortable to tolerate where they are.

Emotionally unavailable people are often unwilling to change because emotions are scary to them and embracing themselves emotionally feels threatening. They believe it's easier not to feel anything even if it makes people around them uncomfortable. In elder parents, lifelong patterns of avoiding emotions create a lot of resistance to change. Remember, you can't force change, but you can use your tools to communicate and interact. You don't have to stay in the same place as your parents, and using your tools can significantly reduce conflict.

In any interaction among or between people, positions are taken that direct how the interactions proceed. I call these positions "emotional locations," and you may find it enlightening to consider them whenever you have an interaction or exchange.

First, a definition: *Emotional location* is the feelings plus action perspective from which a person is operating in any given moment. It's important to note that everyone in an interaction, be it two people or thousands, is operating from an emotional location. The way in which interactions develop has to do with the location your communication partner holds as well as your location. Just to make it seem more complex, people can shift locations in mid-exchange without warning or explanation. Let's make it simpler.

When I use the term "exchange" or "interaction," I'm referring to any verbal or nonverbal communication between or among two to an infinite number of people. It can take place in person, via FaceTime or Skype, by text or email or phone. An exchange can be one-sided, as when you are watching a TV show or film or someone waves as you pass one another, or multisided, like fans at a sporting event or a group conversation. Obviously, within a multisided exchange there can be smaller group exchanges, like those fans discussing a particular call or play.

An exchange can be completely devoid of emotion (Paper or plastic? Fries with that?) or emotionally laden (Teenager: "I hate you. You're the worst mom in the world.") An interaction can be important or trivial. Exchanges or interactions are the foundation of communication and relationships, so the tools of emotional location are very important.

THE FIVE BOXES OF EMOTIONAL LOCATION

Think of this as a grid of communication plus behavior. Of the five boxes, four are dysfunctional. A side note: "dysfunctional" is a really vague term and has been overused. One person's view of dysfunction is another's irritant. When a client comes from a "dysfunctional family," I still have to dig to find out what creates that dysfunction. It might be a big family secret or alcoholism or sexual abuse or drug abuse, or it might be mental illness or poor communication or emotional unavailability. Dysfunctional doesn't define the quality or intensity of what's going on.

"Dysfunctional" is also judgmental. Clients who talk about their "dysfunctional" families or parents often do so from a place of shame as though they are somehow responsible for the behavior of their parents. The only person for whom you can take responsibility is yourself and your behavior and your choices. Everything else occurs around you or sometimes to you but not because of you.

So here's my definition of *dysfunctional* so that we're all operating from the same perspective: *dysfunctional behavior* interferes with growth, clarity of communication, and conflict resolution. This behavior can take place in a relationship, family, or culture. Anything else should have a different, more specific name. When I use the word *dysfunction* in this book, think back on this definition.

Now onto the boxes. The four outlying spots can only be occupied by one person at a time in any exchange or interaction. These are the dysfunctional locations. The center box—the Solver spot—can be occupied by an infinite number of people at any time. Our job in using emotional location is to find a way for everyone in an exchange to occupy the Solver spot together.

People choose their emotional location, and its corresponding behavior, for a reason. Whether you think it's a good or viable reason, it serves a purpose for the person who chooses it. The choice may very well be unconscious, so if you confront a person about her motive for behavioral choices, she may deny it very sincerely because it was not a conscious choice. Emotional location can help you understand these choices and respond appropriately.

Most often, people choose their emotional location in any exchange because it is a position in which they feel safe. For most people, feeling safe means feeling in control. The problem arises when one person's safety or control position is unsafe or out of control to another.

Control is a strong motivator. It's both an internal and external function, physical and psychological. Internally, feeling in control makes a person feel confident, able to make life decisions that will keep his or her world intact. Externally, control often takes the form of seizing power from someone else in order to feel powerful.

Control is gratification-focused: "I will take what I need from you without consideration of what you need or want so I can feel better and stronger. I don't think of what you need or want, only what I need or want." If each person in an exchange is trying to take control, it becomes a battle of wills and everyone involved feels unsafe.

The locations are related to mindsets not only because of the default emotion present in both but also because a person will default to the same location time after time. It's familiar and has predictable results even if it's unhealthy or unsafe. If, as we explore the locations, you recognize yourself as consistently occupying a dysfunctional location and you are aware you're not getting the results you want in interactions, you can make the conscious choice to change. The framework of emotional location not only allows for change but encourages it. Of course, like anything new, it takes practice and understanding to make the change and get comfortable with it. It's a worthy endeavor.

So now let's look at the locations, their relationship, and why they work—or don't.

The Solver

We'll start with the ideal location. The Solver position welcomes an infinite number of participants who are seeking to solve a problem equitably. The Solver spot is the one in which a person feels competent, able, and open. It's respectful to all persons involved; is focused on the problem, not the person; and is looking for solution not gratification.

Solvers . . .

✓ Focus on the problem, not the person
✓ Are respectful
✓ Seek a solution, not gratification
✓ Empower everyone in an exchange
✓ Are assertive, not aggressive
✓ Seek win-win resolutions
✓ Are emotionally available
✓ Have good boundaries
✓ Communicate clearly and purposefully

The key to being a Solver is being solution-focused. What that means is the exchange is focused on one problem and its solution. The exchange should not wander into personalities, history, or other problems. There should be no attempt to find someone to be wrong or "bad" or at fault. Instead, the exchange is focused on finding the best solution to a single problem in which everyone involved can feel empowered and everyone wins.

Respectful treatment of others cannot be overemphasized. I'll give you an example. You have ordered something on the Internet, and when it arrives, it's not at all what you'd hoped for or expected. Fortunately, the company has a customer service phone line. So you call. And you're on hold listening alternately to music you don't like and an announcement about how important you are to XYZ Buggywhip if you just continue to hold. Your aggravation level rises so that by the time the customer service person takes your call, you are full-on mad. You have come to the point of a choice. You can blow up at the customer service person and demand to know why they screwed up your order, as though they personally did it just to inconvenience you, *or* you can explain the situation respectfully and together seek a solution. Ask yourself which path will be more likely to bring you what you want.

Yelling at the only person in a position to solve your problem is gratification-focused and aggressive. Gratification-focused exchanges occur when people are focused on getting their own needs met, regardless of what the other person needs or wants. Gratification-focused interactions have little to do with solving problems. Rather, the clear message is, I want what I want, and I don't care if you get hurt or lose in the process.

Solvers seek to empower themselves and others and realize they can only control themselves and their own behavior. A Solver is not seeking to take control of someone else or of the situation but rather to find a mutually agreeable resolution. Ultimately, control is keeping your own power and allowing everyone else in the exchange to do the same. Empowerment is important to finding a solution because everyone involved needs to feel that their voices and ideas are being heard and considered.

A Solver, solution-focused, empowering response is assertive. Being assertive means you clearly ask for what you need but in a respectful and solution-focused manner. "I'd like to go to the concert. I hear you say you'd rather go to a movie. What do we need to do to solve this problem?" You have asked for what you want, acknowledged the position of the other person, and asked for resolution. That's being assertive.

Aggressive, on the other hand, sounds like, "Well, I don't want to go to that stupid movie. I want to go to the concert and you're going with me." In general, aggressive behavior is gratification-focused and looks only to satisfy the needs of the aggressive person.

A win-win resolution doesn't necessarily mean everyone gets everything they want. Instead, it's a product of compromise. Using the example of the concert vs. the movie above, a win-win compromise would sound like, "How about if we go to the concert tonight since it's only one night and go to the movie on Friday since it will still be in the theater then?" Both parties' interests are acknowledged and included, so both get some of what they want and give up a bit, in this case in timing.

Being emotionally available means not trying to take control or force a particular position but rather to listen carefully not only to what is being said but the emotions behind it and then respond appropriately. It means having an awareness of the feelings of everyone involved and incorporating those feelings into the resolution if at all possible or addressing those feelings in explaining potential solutions.

We've talked about boundaries and the importance of having them and respecting other's boundaries. Boundaries are an essential for Solvers. Signs of bad boundaries are being aggressive, gratification-focused, blaming, demanding, and abusive. Good boundaries include respect, kindness, consideration, thoughtfulness, and good communication. Good boundaries create the perfect environment for finding solutions.

Finally, good communication is the essential key to being a Solver. Good communication involves both speaking and listening. When speaking, it's important to say what you mean clearly and respectfully, and sticking to a maximum of three sentences before yielding the floor. When listening, keep eye contact and be attentive. Use "I feel" language. Respond, don't react.

Now we'll consider the four "dysfunctional" locations and how to move people from those positions to being a Solver.

The Blamer

Everyone has had experience with a Blamer: a person who accuses everyone else of being the source of a problem. Everything the Blamer says is accompanied by the visible or implied shaking finger of shame. The Blamer's objective is to make others feel unworthy, unable, inept, and in short, abused. In this way the Blamer feels more complete, more powerful, and more in control.

Control is key to understanding the motives of the Blamers. Their approach to gathering power is to use manipulation, attacks, and condemnation. Blamers tend to use hyperbole to attack someone else. Their accusations are laden with phrases like "the very worst," "totally incompetent," and "completely inferior." They also spread shame with words like "should," "always," "never," "fault," and "if," as in "If you weren't so totally incompetent...."

Blamers are not looking for a solution to a problem. They are looking for someone to be wrong so that they can feel superior because someone else being wrong means they are right. They want not only to assign blame for events going awry but also to make people the problem rather than making the problem the problem. Obviously, if you don't focus on the problem, finding a solution is impossible.

"I told you six months ago you were wrong about having this party for your father's birthday and now it turns out I was right because you chose to have it on the day of the worst weather of any April in memory. But you had to have it your way and you are, as usual, incompetent."

You can't defend yourself because the accusation is irrational. How could you, or anyone for that matter, have predicted there would be bad weather on the day of the party, especially six months out? Not to mention you shouldn't have to defend yourself for doing something nice and loving for your dad. There is no mention of a problem to be solved, leaving you powerless.

Blamers choose this aggressive style to accomplish a couple of things. First, they feel better and more powerful when they can push someone into a submissive position.

A side note: There is an important difference between *submission* and *surrender*. Submission is an involuntary position that takes your power away. For example, people who are incarcerated are in a submissive position. They didn't choose to be in prison and don't have control over their lives. Surrender, on the other hand, arises as a result of choice. As an example, when I get on an airplane, I am choosing to trust the pilots to be experts and I surrender my control of the flight experience to the pilots and crew. I retain my personal power because I have made the choice to be there and *choice = power*. When a Blamer attacks, the intent is to take your personal power—your choice—away by putting you in the position of being responsible, not for the solution of a problem, but for being the problem.

Choice = Power

A second mission of the Blamer is trying to take control of you and the situation by creating fear. It can be fear of a physical assault or an emotional assault. If your parent is a Blamer, the not-so-subtle message you get is not only that you are the problem but also that being the problem makes you unlovable and worthy of derision or abandonment.

This often takes the form of "you're not good enough to deserve my love or respect" and is a powerful emotional assault, particularly for kids. These kids then grow into adulthood believing they are not worthy of anyone's love or respect or kindness, creating relationship problems, low self-esteem, negative self-talk, and potentially, mental health issues.

No one wants to feel he or she is, by virtue of being, the problem. The emotional result of being identified as the problem comes down to feeling shame. Guilt is something a person feels as a result of something he or she has done. It's prompted by behavior or choices made.

Shame, on the other hand, isn't focused on behavior but rather on the person. The message of shame is that you as a person are bad. Shame undermines self-confidence. It's a power-down position, and that reduction of power is what allows the Blamer to feel more powerful or stronger.

Guilt comes from bad choices.
Shame comes from being told you are a bad person.

In the party example, the Blamer wants to make it clear that not only was the blamed person responsible for the weather being bad but the blamed person is bad, not for behavior or choices but for simply being.

The Blamer remains emotionally unavailable by distributing shame and blame to keep others off balance. Being in a relationship with a Blamer means not only constantly having to defend yourself against continuing attacks for simply being but also being stripped of your power at every opportunity. It's exhausting and soul depleting.

Parents who get into a Blamer mode with their kids focus on the negative and ignore the positive choices their kids make. If questioned, the frequent reply is that by focusing on the negative, the child will learn not to make the same mistake again. They fear the child will grow up to be lazy or arrogant if they praise the positive behavior. On the other hand, parents who focus only on the positive are not giving their kids an accurate picture of how the world works. The "everybody gets a trophy" approach doesn't teach kids how to manage disappointment. We talk more about that a bit later.

It's important to both praise and criticize—constructively. Harsh criticism or personal attacks are not constructive and deliver the message that the child is unlovable and unloved. Constructive criticism sounds like, "I believe you wanted to do the right thing. Can we talk about other choices you might have made?" Too much praise delivers the message that the child's only value is what he can do, not who he is. Overpraising sounds like, "Billy, you are the best kid on your team. Actually, you're probably the best shortstop in the state. Nobody is any better than you." Balance in all things . . .

> ### Blamers . . .
>
> ✓ Shame
> ✓ Are self-gratifying
> ✓ Focus on the person, not the problem
> ✓ Look for someone to be wrong so that they can be right
> ✓ Avoid being responsible
> ✓ Are aggressive and attacking
> ✓ Take power away
> ✓ Want to be in control
> ✓ Manipulate and create fear

The Poor Me

The Poor Me is the Blamer's usual partner. The Blamer says, "It's all your fault because of who you are." The Poor Me agrees. "It is my fault. You're right. I never do anything right. I am completely hopeless, bad, wrong, a terrible person, *but* it's really not my fault because I am your victim." The Blamer doesn't want to accept responsibility and certainly doesn't want to be seen as a victimizer, so the Blamer deflects the blame back to a criticism of the Poor Me, attempting to reestablish the wrongness of the Poor Me as a person. The Poor Me's position is that, although it may be true she is a bad, unlovable, terrible person, it's not really her fault because it's the Blamer's fault. And, as the exchange devolves, the dynamic changes and the Blamer and the Poor Me switch positions.

The Blamers' tool of choice is fear with the objective to seize control. The Poor Me's tool is helplessness, waiting passively for others to read their mind and come to the rescue. The helplessness is a chosen position, hence a power position, designed to maintain control. The thinking is that if you're helpless, wrong, and powerless, how can you possibly be responsible? Not only that, but if you're helpless, wrong, and powerless, you are also emotionally unavailable, so you don't have to risk being vulnerable.

The Blamer says it's the Poor Me's fault, and if the Poor Me had only listened to the Blamer, whatever the terrible event is would never have happened, but because the Poor Me is a bad person and didn't listen, the fault lies completely with the Poor Me. The Poor Me doesn't want to be responsible for anything so pushes the blame to another or to uncontrollable events. What neither party recognizes is, in virtually all cases, assigning blame is a waste of time. Such recognition would be uncomfortable for the Blamer because if there is no one to blame, the Blamer couldn't take power away. The Poor Me is uncomfortable with no blame because then there is nothing to deflect.

Poor Mes have trouble recognizing themselves emotionally without an external definition. In a situation in which blame is assigned, there is a clear definition. Blamers have trouble recognizing themselves emotionally because they don't feel the power surge of connection as they are taking the power of the other. Both are desperate to avoid taking responsibility.

The Poor Me, to some degree, believes he deserves to be blamed. It's a circular logic: "I deserve to be abused because I'm a bad person, but I'm a bad person because I was abused." This circle blocks emotional availability, solution-focus, or healthy relationships. It is also self-reinforcing.

There are times the Poor Me will initiate negative exchanges with the Blamer in an attempt to make an emotional connection with the Blamer, no matter how unhealthy or nonproductive. It is, however, familiar.

Remember, the relationship between the Blamer and the Poor Me is intense, enmeshed, and potentially volatile. The roles, as I pointed out before, often flip back and forth, with the Blamer taking the Poor Me role and the Poor Me becoming the Blamer.

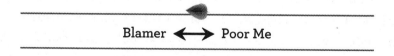

Blamer ←→ Poor Me

The Blamer/Poor Me relationship is the classic abuse relationship.

This pattern is, unfortunately, common. The relationship is burdened with rules and expectations, many of them impossible or at least unreasonable and most unspoken. Any deviation from those expectations and rules produces chaos in the relationship and starts the blame/shame cycle. Not only does the Blamer want to control the Poor Me, but the Blamer also wants to punish the Poor Me and needs the Poor Me to accept the punishment. This not only reinforces the belief in the Poor Me that she is the problem but gives the sense of connection, no matter how dysfunctional.

The Blamer may get power by striking out physically but then is burdened with shame and guilt. The Blamer then must find a place to unload these uncomfortable feelings, and you can imagine who becomes the target, perpetuating the cycle of victimization while still giving both partners some of what they need emotionally.

This abusive relationship is volatile and can be passionate with lots of yelling and turmoil, emotion and drama. There is always the potential for violence.

Poor Mes . . .

✓ Control through helplessness
✓ Focus on perceived victimization
✓ Seek to deflect responsibility
✓ Switches positions with the Blamer

The Fixer

Moving to the other side of the outlying boxes, we find the Fixer. The Fixer's attempt to control comes through intrusive action. The Fixer's message is, essentially, "I know more about what you need than you do so I'm going to do it/get it/fix it for you, no matter what you may say you want and no matter how mad you might feel." This is caretaking with a whip and a chair!

**Taking care is doing something
for someone they are unable to do for themselves.
Caretaking is doing something for someone they
can and should do for themselves.**

Unlike the Blamer, who tries to take control by fear and manipulation, or the Poor Me, who tries to control through helplessness, the Fixer controls with the illusion of kindness while smothering and enfolding the other person. The Fixer's control style is aggressive caring reinforced by guilt. Lots and lots of guilt.

Let me give you an example. My mom was staying at our house while we were on vacation, taking care of our dogs and visiting her friends in our area. While here she decided she didn't like the way our kitchen was arranged and completely reorganized it to her liking. Now, more than twenty-five years later, there are still things I can't find. I suspect she may have thrown them away.

How is this being a Fixer? First, she didn't ask if we wanted the kitchen reorganized and then got huffy with me when I asked her to help me understand her decision to do this. Second, she arranged the kitchen the way she wanted it, not the way it worked for us. Finally she revealed she felt as though we weren't grateful enough for her dog sitting even though we thanked her profusely, brought her gifts from the trip, and most important, she had insisted on doing it!

Fixers use guilt to tip the balance of power in their direction. The Fixer sounds as though he is victimizing himself for the good of others, but that's an illusion. The Fixer's real objective is to take control by offering what looks like caring. The message is, "I've done this for you, so now you owe me." Those debts are impossible to repay because the Fixer will create a new debt before you can resolve the last one.

Fixers smother. Their attempts at fixing extend far beyond assistance or problem solving since no problem is identified and the result is often chaos and enmeshment because the Fixer is always the center of the "solution" even when it isn't a solution at all. The essence of the message of the Fixer is, "I am the answer."

The real need of the Fixer is to feel loved. Fixers will do whatever they think it takes to get the love they so desperately need and have never felt to a satisfying degree.

The language of the Fixer revolves around phrases like "your needs," "protect you," "help you." None of these phrases is related to a Solver's offer of help or kindness as part of a solution to a problem because if you listen carefully, you will clearly hear the strings attached: In order for the needs, help, or protection to occur, it must be on the Fixer's terms and comes with a debt. They get power and control because they see you in a submissive position by virtue of their actions. Remember, a debt is always created.

"You spent our rent money at the casino? From now on, I'll manage our money and I'll get an extra job and you don't have to worry about it because I can make this all right again." That might sound like help until you listen to how much power is being siphoned away to the Fixer. The Fixer is putting herself into a control position as well as creating an obligation. The sense of caring isn't caring; it's controlling. If the Fixee doesn't perform exactly as the Fixer outlines, guilt will result. The Fixer is attempting to feel safe, needed, and loved by taking control. The often-resulting chaos is interpreted by the Fixer as further evidence of their need to control.

Sometimes the Fixer resorts to physical violence but not as a means of gaining control. It would arise from frustration. The Fixer's perspective is "If you don't let me take care of you and then love me for it, I'll hurt you." The frustration usually arises from resistance to control by the Fixee.

Fixers . . .

✓ Control with "kindness"
✓ Are intrusive
✓ Distribute guilt
✓ Offer helpfulness as a cloak for control
✓ Believe "I am the answer"
✓ Create an obligation that can never be repaid

In general, the Fixer's primary relationship in the grid will be with the Player.

The Player

Players focus on themselves and their needs to the exclusion of others. They don't care who gets hurt or makes sacrifices as long as they get what they want. Often Players are alcoholic, drug addicted, gamblers, overspenders, unreliable, or narcissistic. The Player controls by manipulation and carelessness. "If you love me, you'll make this right." This attitude is coupled with a subtler message: "If you're perfect, I might love you," but perfect is never defined and the real operable word is "might."

Players are always emotionally unavailable. They may be able to pretend to be connected for a while, but it's a façade and an intellectual exercise, not real emotion. The façade and the subtle message are the perfect bait for the Fixer who believes he or she can be perfect enough to win the love of the Player . . . and control the Player.

Players are very skilled at emotional seduction. Early in the relationship the façade is firmly in place and they appear to be loving and connected, attentive and ready to fill every need of the partner. Invariably, however, they cannot sustain the façade and will use any event or disagreement to shift to demanding more and giving less. The Fixer then becomes frightened of losing the Player, so fixes and caretakes more in an effort to bring back the loving and connected Player. That person no longer exists and never did in the first place.

Meanwhile, the Fixer works harder and harder to fix, make better, control with kindness, and manage the behavior of the Player, ostensibly for the Player's own good. The seduction becomes the illusion that the Fixer can somehow unlock the "real" emotional self of the Player.

What does the Player get from all this? Everything. The Fixer does all the work in the relationship while the Player sits back and waits for the Fixer to deliver. When the Fixer doesn't deliver—and no matter what the Fixer does, it will never be enough—the Player then has someone to blame for his problem; someone who won't leave but will instead try harder to keep giving them exactly what they want.

Underlying the Player's emotional unavailability is a deeply buried insecurity, a fear of abandonment, and a belief they can't really take care of themselves. Under the Fixer's guilt and control needs is a feeling of not being good enough and therefore not lovable and only accepted for what they can do, not who they are.

These are the hooks that anchor the relationship. The Fixer tries to earn the love of the Player by attempting to read the Player's mind and providing what the Player needs perfectly. The Player believes she needs someone to do things and create feelings because he or she is unable to do that. Players, however, do not allow anyone to get close emotionally because vulnerability is dangerous and might lead to abandonment.

The Player/Fixer relationship is classic codependence, and the energy flow, rather than being the place-changing of the Blamer/Poor Me, always goes from Fixer to Player.

Fixer ➤ Player

Players often sound apologetic and contrite, deflecting responsibility—which they will never take—to someone else who "took advantage of" them.

They will frequently begin an excuse with, "Yes, but . . ." Keep in mind, *the word "but" erases everything that came before it.* Therefore, "yes, but . . ." actually means no. The Fixer-Player relationship is the relationship of addiction.

Players never take responsibility for their behavior and choices. It is always someone else's fault, and the Player is always the victim. Fixers want so desperately to be loved that they will do everything possible to repair the damages, even taking responsibility for the Player's choices. Of course, it's never quite perfect enough for the Player, but that's what keeps the relationship rolling.

Players . . .

✓ Control with manipulation
✓ Are evasive
✓ Are irresponsible
✓ Are emotionally unavailable
✓ Use "Yes, but . . ." to deflect responsibility
✓ Seduce emotionally with a façade
✓ Are often narcissists, addicts, cheaters

The Fixer/Player relationship is as entrenched as that of the Blamer/Poor Me, but rather than yelling and violence, the interaction is more often characterized by tears and power struggles. The Fixer and Player do not switch but are instead locked into their respective roles.

Do any of these locations feel familiar? Did you cringe when you read any of the descriptions? It's important to recognize if you are locked into or frequently occupy any place other than the Solver spot.

Remember, everyone jumps in and out of emotional locations all the time. If you find yourself and your parent or child stuck in a particular location and pattern, you can choose to jump into the Solver spot. Be warned: Going to and staying in the Solver spot takes practice and determination. The benefits of staying in the Solver spot are immense. It becomes an effective way to navigate all areas of life, reduce stress, create bonds with others, and virtually eliminate conflict.

OTHER CONNECTIONS IN THE GRID

The Blamer/Poor Me and Fixer/Player relationships exist in all human interactions, not just family or intimate partners. Those are the primary connections, but there are other possibilities that put the "dys" in dysfunction.

Blamer/Player

The key to understanding this possible relationship is to remember that Blamers want to gain control by assigning blame and shame for anything to their partners, not because of behavior but because of whom they are. The Player wants to find someone to take responsibility for things that go wrong and to avoid being blamed. Oil and water!

Blamers might jump into the Fixer spot to add guilt to the shame they distribute, but their intention is not to fix anything. The Player might jump over to the Poor Me spot with the "Yes, but I did that because it's your fault" approach, but the Player lacks the emotional connection to feel shame. The whole objective is to shift blame for behavior to someone else.

Players want to use people to avoid having to solve problems for themselves. Blamers are not at all interested in being used. Players manipulate by pretending to feel emotions. Blamers manipulate by taking control and instilling fear. Players, disconnected from their feelings, don't experience guilt or fear and do all they can to avoid being responsible.

You can see how little likelihood this relationship would have of forming or surviving.

Blamer/Fixer

In a possible Blamer/Fixer relationship, problems would quickly arise because both want to be in control. The Blamer's control efforts of blame/

shame/fear conflict with the Fixer's control approach of guilt/obligation. Blamers lash out at the smothering control efforts of the Fixer and reject the guilt attempts. This might push the Fixer into the Poor Me position, a spot familiar to a Fixer who filled that role in the family of origin.

Children of the abuse cycle of the Blamer/Poor Me get the message early that they must be in charge of fixing things for their parents. They become the referees, peacemakers, or Fixers in the family. As they become adults, they extend their fixing to others from whom they are trying, often futilely, to get love. These frustrated Fixers have been blamed by their Blamer/Poor Me parents for not being good enough to fix the unfixable relationship of the parents. In adulthood they try to find other unfixables to reinforce their assigned role as failure, and they will fail again.

The Blamer doesn't want to be fixed, nor does the Poor Me. Their relationship is based on the chaos of the abusive tornado they live in, and they prefer to keep it that way. The attempts of the child Fixer to resolve the complex and enmeshed parental Blamer/Poor Me relationship are destined to be unsuccessful not only because the participants don't want to be fixed but also because kids don't have the skill set to untangle such a mess. The Blamer, however, pushes the child into the Fixer role with assertions that the child is part of the problem and therefore should be able to fix it. This is *never* true. The child never had a role in creating the abusive relationship of the adults nor does the child have the ability to resolve it.

Fixer/Poor Me

You'd think this might be a primary connection but the relationship between a Fixer and a Poor Me doesn't work primarily because Poor Mes are not really looking for something to be fixed, particularly themselves. The Poor Me believes he is unfixable, so anyone who tries to help or fix is viewed as intrusive, crazy, or untrustworthy. The Poor Me doesn't want things to be fixed because then he would have to take some responsibility for how his life goes. Instead, the Poor Me is happy continuing to feel hopeless and helpless with the Blamer to reinforce those feelings because although they are uncomfortable, they are familiar.

The message of the Fixer is that everyone can be fixed if only they will submit and give their power to the Fixer. Poor Mes don't believe they have any power to give up nor anything of value to fix, so the smothering of the Fixer is frightening. In neither case is there a real connection. Instead, the Poor Me retreats and may jump into the Blamer spot to make the Fixer go away.

The Poor Me looks like a good target to the Fixer, particularly since Players sometimes use Poor Me language to further seduce the Fixer. "I know I blew the rent money at the casino. I really thought I was going to hit it big, but you know my luck. I am such a failure and you're so strong." The Player doesn't really take responsibility nor offer to take part in the resolution of the issue. Instead he blames bad luck—a true intangible—and reinforces the power of the Fixer to resolve the problem. The Fixer hears the "compliment" and rushes to live up to it.

The Poor Me, on the other hand, sticks with self-blaming. "I'm an awful person and because I'm an awful person I make awful choices. I don't know why you would ever want to help me because I will just screw up again." These words might sound like Fixer bait and might work for a while with the Fixer but the implication of the correctness of the Poor Me's self-assessment herself will eventually cause the Fixer not to get the fixing rush being sought. The Poor Me won't be grateful, just self-blaming.

Player/Poor Me

The other possible secondary connection would be Player/Poor Me. It might sound like a natural connection because the Player is looking for someone to blame and the Poor Me is an expert at being blamed. What doesn't work is that the Player wants more than just a blame target; she wants someone to pick up the pieces, and the Poor Me doesn't function like that.

The Player says, "It's your fault." The Poor Me agrees. Then nothing happens, so the Player doesn't get the secondary gain of making someone else responsible and again blames the Poor Me, who agrees and again nothing happens. The Player, in order to make those demands visible, continues to escalate, and the Poor Me, frustrated, eventually jumps into the Blamer spot, driving the Player away. It's also possible the Player will jump into the Blamer spot and use physical violence to express frustration with the Poor Me. In neither case is there a connection.

The Player doesn't get the problem resolved and the Poor Me gets exactly what is expected: to be the one at fault. Meanwhile, the initial problem continues to exist to the frustration of both parties.

Two people trying to occupy the same outlying locations will be equally unsuccessful. Remember, each of the outlying locations can only be occupied by one person at a time. If two people try to hold the same place, power struggles will ensue for sure, and one of the two will relocate.

GETTING TO THE SOLVER SPOT

None of the outlying locations is solution-focused. All those locations are seeking gratification of one kind or another. There is no awareness of the emotions or needs of the others involved in the exchanges.

If you are in one of these patterns and you are ready to change, there is a way to derail the dysfunctional connections and build healthier relationships.

Let's say your dad is a Blamer. As far back as you can remember, most of what comes out of his mouth is blame and shame, most often directed at your mom but also at everyone around him, including you.

"You must be the stupidest woman who ever lived. Any idiot could figure this out but you're not just any idiot. You and your stupid son will be the death of me. He's just an incompetent fool."

What did you feel when you read that? What did you want to say in response? The temptation would be either to shrink into a tiny little ball of Poor Me and agree with Dad—you are an incompetent fool—or to jump into the Blamer spot and attack him with the same sort of language and vigor. You might also try the Fixer approach, particularly to care for your mom, or you might adopt the emotionless blame shifting of the Player. Any of those choices will keep you firmly in the dysfunctional, non-solution-focused place where nothing gets solved and chaos rules.

If you stop and think for a minute, there is probably nothing you could say to change Dad's mind or his approach if you respond as victim or with venom because he's feeling good for making you feel bad.

However, if you can move into the Solver spot, you absolutely can and will make a difference. So how do you manage that miracle? Easy. You use Bryn's Six Magic Words.

BRYN'S SIX MAGIC WORDS:
"I'm sorry you feel that way."

Imagine for a moment responding with the Six Magic Words to your dad's abusive tirade—not in a snotty or disrespectful way, but with eye contact and courtesy. You are, indeed, sorry he feels that way. You respectfully disagree and decline to engage in an abusive conversation.

When delivered in a respectful tone, these are powerful words, which should be followed immediately by Bryn's Magic Question:

BRYN'S MAGIC QUESTION:
"What do we need to do to solve this problem?"

This question accomplishes a lot of objectives in changing the texture of the exchange. First, you're refusing to engage in dysfunctional behavior. Second, you're being clear you will not tolerate abuse. Third, you are asking the Blamer, in this case, to identify a problem as the problem, not a person as the problem. Fourth, you are inviting the Blamer to join you in problem solving. Finally, you are moving away from gratification-focus to a problem-solving focus.

It would be lovely if this would work the first time—or even the first hundred times—you say the Magic Words and ask the Magic Question. You will probably initially hear Dad say, "The problem, Son, is you are stupid and so is your mother. Fix that!"

Don't relent. "Dad, I don't believe Mom or I am the problem. I think together you and I need to identify the problem we want to solve and then work on solving it without blaming anyone." Be firm, keep your boundaries tight, look him in the eye, and keep the anger out of your voice.

Be creative. You can find equivalent Magic Words that fit comfortably in your mouth and mind. Some suggestions would be:

"Thanks for your input. I would like for us to identify a problem so we can solve it."

"Thank you for telling me how you feel. Is there a problem we can try to solve?"

"I see you feel strongly about this. Can we identify a problem and work to solve it?"

"I'd like for us to find a way to work together to solve this problem."

You get the idea. The essence of the message is that you acknowledge Dad and his expressed feelings but you will not get enmeshed in his dysfunctional position. You are clear you are focused on identifying a problem—not a person to blame—and solving that problem. This will require persistence, patience, and practice. You may have times during which you can't have conversations with Dad because he is persisting in being abusive. Or, if you are having nonabusive conversations and they suddenly become abusive, use the Magic Words, ask the Magic Question, give him a chance to change, and if he doesn't, respectfully walk away.

Similar Magic Words work within the Fixer/Player relationship. The Player says, "I blew the rent money at the casino." This is bait for the Fixer to step up and fix. Instead, use a version of the Six Magic Words, like, "That's troubling," or "This really creates a problem for us," or "I'm really disappointed to hear that." Stay calm, cool, and collected. Don't yell or cry, and most of all, don't fix. Then ask the Magic Question.

The Player will do what Players do: either blame someone else—probably the Fixer—and then pout or storm out. As with dealing with the Blamer, don't relent and do ask for what you need. Again, it may take a bunch of trials to engage the Player in the problem solving, or you may decide you've had enough and walk away. In either case, you will keep your power in the Solver spot.

The Solver spot is the ultimate power position for everyone involved. Identifying and solving problems feels good. It's an accomplishment. The trick is getting people who are stuck in dysfunctional positions to join you so that they can feel that sense of accomplishment as well. The Solver spot leads to spending less emotional energy because you don't need to constantly defend yourself. Instead you can spend your emotional energy on creating healthy connections.

The Solver spot, remember, can be occupied by an infinite number of people. Once you learn how to stay in the Solver spot, you will find the chaos in your life drops dramatically. There will still be conflicts—you're human—but because you know how to pull people into the Solver position, they are apt to be healthy, growing, and quickly resolved. Good communication skills are at the heart of healthy emotional connections.

Good communication allows us to clearly express our feelings and our thoughts. In my practice, it's clear that people's communication skills are learned in childhood. If parents are poor at communicating, the kids will be poor communicators, who then grow up to be parents who are poor at expressing themselves.

COMMUNICATION SKILLS

There are some basics to good communication: practice, practice, practice. Nobody is ever perfect at communication, but if you make a mistake, own it and correct it as soon as possible. The more you use good communication skills, the better your communication becomes and the more able you are to stay in the Solver spot and have others join you there. Good communication is a powerful tool to overcome emotional unavailability with parents and children, as well as with the rest of the world.

Change is not something you can inflict on someone else. A parent who is emotionally unavailable must be willing to change. As you use your communication skills, however, they may recognize the value and benefit to making changes and you can reinforce such a realization.

Remember, the more you stay in the Solver spot, not only with your emotionally unavailable parent but also with the world in general, you will lower your stress level and raise your effectiveness. Being in the Solver spot keeps you away from no-win conflicts. You will avoid those circular, going-nowhere communications that only serve to leave all involved anxious, mad, and without solutions.

So here are the fundamental building blocks of good communication:

Use "I Feel" Language

We covered this pretty thoroughly in the beginning of this chapter, so this is just a reminder. Please also remember the three-sentence rule.

Ask Open-Ended Questions

An open-ended question is one that cannot be answered with some version of "yes" or "no" or the dreaded and totally ineffective "I don't know." Open-ended questions make it harder for your parent or child to stonewall you.

For example, a closed-ended question would be, "Are you mad at me?" (which is a terrible question, by the way). The open-ended version of the same question would be, "You appear to feel mad. Please help me understand." When you are dealing with someone who's emotionally unavailable, you may have to find several ways to ask the same question because your obviously angry parent will try to dodge making an explanation. Don't get discouraged. Stay with Solver language. "If you can help me identify the problem, we can work together on a solution." "I would like to hear your perspective on this issue so we can work together to find a solution to the problem."

Use open-ended questions in conjunction with "I feel" language and stick with it.

Set Clear Boundaries

We talked about the importance of boundaries. Good communication requires strong boundaries, particularly with people who are abusive or blaming or who refuse to participate in a reasonable dialog.

If you have tried multiple times in multiple ways to engage your parent or child in a solution-focused discussion and you have realized an unwillingness or inability to change, you have a problem beyond communication. That doesn't mean you can abandon your efforts at clear communication. You have the right to be heard and to have your feelings treated respectfully. If you are repeatedly rebuffed in your efforts, you may want to limit the relationship, particularly if there is abusive language or behavior.

Break Down the Problem

Sometimes people try to solve a complex problem with an all in one solution. While tempting, this is really impossible. Complex problems are complex for a reason, and usually the reason is that people have ignored the little, more solvable issues that have wound themselves into a *problem*.

Try to reduce the problem to its smallest parts and resolve those one at a time. Breaking the issue down can be a key to resolution. It's more work, but it may get you the results you desire.

Tyrone and his dad, Walter, have rarely seen eye to eye on almost any issue. Walter, an attorney, likes to argue and sees it almost as recreation. He also has a strong need to be right. Tyrone, a successful financial planner, prefers resolution and compromise. Over the years they have argued intensely about politics, religion, money, career choices, colleges, sports, and even game shows. Felicia, Tyrone's mom and Walter's wife, retreats from the room when they start, preferring time with the other kids to listening to her son and husband fight.

While many of their disagreements can be easily dismissed, several themes—money, career choices, colleges—have recurred and been unresolved over time. These unfinished conflicts had become a messy tangle when they came to my office. After several sessions in which each complained about the behavior of the other, I introduced them to emotional location and asked each to identify where they spent the most time when they were together and when they were apart.

Tyrone responded quickly. "When I'm not with Dad, I'm a Solver. I like being in the Solver position and identifying a problem, then solving it.

When I'm with Dad, I think I tend to get into the Blamer/Poor Me cycle."

Walter was thoughtful. "That's funny, because I think the same thing. In my practice, I have to be the Solver. That's why my clients are paying me. But I get around Tyrone and we get into that abusive cycle. I think I'm probably more of a Blamer and he's more of a Poor Me." He paused, then added, "I think Tyrone being a Poor Me and just taking my . . . uh . . . abuse makes me mad. I want him to fight back like he did when he went to college. I told him I wanted him to be a lawyer and take over my firm. He didn't argue with me so I thought we agreed. Turned out he majored in finance. I didn't know until he was going into his senior year and I asked him when he was taking the LSAT. He told me he wasn't. He was going to grad school to get an MBA." He turned to Tyrone. "I was really proud of you, but I was also mad."

Tyrone nodded. "I was so scared to tell you. I knew you were mad. So I decided not to argue with you about it. Truthfully, I still resent your assumption I would blindly follow your path."

I asked, "Would you consider that one piece of the *problem*?"

Both men nodded.

"So what do we need to do to solve this particular problem? First, identify it."

Tyrone said, "I think the problem is I felt controlled and as though I didn't have the right to make my own choices. Dad wasn't paying for my education—I was on a full ride for baseball—but he thought he could define my life and my interests."

Walter looked surprised. "I thought the problem was Tyrone was lying to me."

We found out the problem was hard to solve because it was different in each of their eyes. So we ended up solving two problems. This pattern continued as we worked our way through the *problem*, one—usually two—problems at a time.

Do not allow your boundaries to be violated. If there is abusive language or behavior, confront it immediately, not in a hostile or upset way, but with clear language and communication of feelings. "I feel attacked by you when you call me names. This is not okay with me. If you can't communicate without abusive language, I'm going to end this discussion and leave." They may agree, and you need to be willing to leave. Don't let your mouth write a check your body won't cash!

Practice, Practice, Practice

This speaks for itself!

PART TWO

Difficult Parents

Remember, your relationship with your difficult parent(s) has a deep foundation and a lot of accumulated experience backing it up. Rather than trying to fix all the historical difficulties at once—because that will *never* work—focus on what's happening now.

Also remember, if the problem parent(s) are elderly, they are much less likely to make sweeping changes—or even little ones. As people get older, their emotional positions tend to become fixed at the same time their social veneers begin to fall away. This stubbornness and lack of social filters make it harder for them to hear constructive criticism and make changes. Your job becomes one of recognition, using the tools from Parts 1 and 3 and not letting yourself get sucked into their drama to help you feel less burdened and less guilty. Difficult parents are often masters of distributing guilt, and your job is not to accept it. It's the gift you don't want and have the clear option not to accept.

Finally, when looking at these categories, please remember these things:

- Nobody fits the categories perfectly. They're general overviews.
- Some difficult parents exhibit a combination of types, compounding your problems dealing with them.
- Do one thing at a time and remind yourself that their plans do not create obligations for you. You have the right to say yes or no. Both are complete sentences.
- Don't play their games. They are really good at what they do and have been doing it for a long time. The realization you don't have to participate is powerful. The only way to win is not to play.
- Exhibit compassion without getting sucked in to sympathy. Compassion is the ability to feel what others might feel in a particular situation. Sympathy, on the other hand, is taking on the burdens of

others without keeping your boundaries tight. Essentially sympathy is codependent. Sympathy is also condescending because it comes from a place where one person feels superior to the other. It's not a constructive position.

- Boundaries, boundaries, boundaries, boundaries.
- Use good, clear, effective communication.
- Remember to be a Solver and encourage others to join you in that spot.

4

Inconsistent Parents

Inconsistency is a trust violation and includes behaviors like lying or manipulation and then alternately cheerleading even when there's not much to cheer about. One day they're tyrants, the next they're almost indifferent. One day there are impossible rules to follow, the next, no rules at all. We like people to be predictable. Parents who are not predictable create trust issues.

As the adult child of an inconsistent parent, you are always off-balance, never knowing from day to day what to expect. Will Mom want to see her grandkids and enjoy the day with them or will she make them clean her house? Will Dad be on one of his tirades about politics where he yells and scares the kids or will he be the mellow guy who wants to build a castle with Legos? By the time you get to them you're tense and prepared for the worst, or you decide to be optimistic and get blindsided.

Inconsistency also shows up as broken promises. Far too often I hear adult children of inconsistent parents talk with great sadness and anger about a parent who made promises they did not keep.

"For your birthday, we're going to take the whole family to Disney World." Not even to the local McDonald's.

"On Saturday, you and I will spend the whole day together, just the two of us." And the new girlfriend and her kids.

"I know you love the American Girl dolls, and remember, Christmas is coming." With no American Girl doll.

"We'll go to at least ten ball games this summer." Or none.

Children hear things like this as promises and so they attach to them and remember them. They take on life and energy. Disney World, special time together with the parent, a much-coveted doll, or ball games become the basis for hopeful fantasies. While an adult might hear the proposed plan as possible, the child hears it as a promise, and when that promise is ignored, along with many others offered in the same casual way, trust is broken and hurts build up. That accumulation of hurts, slights, and broken promises erodes the parent-child relationship.

If you are the child of an inconsistent parent who has broken promises, the best gift you can give yourself is to be reliable to yourself. For example, New Year's resolutions seem made to be broken. The average person makes a promise—often involving exercise, weight loss, or spending habits—and then shrugs three weeks later when those promises have fallen prey to the cold months of winter and the depression of postholiday letdown. For someone who's been given promises by parents that didn't happen, broken self-promises are painful and can contribute to depression.

This doesn't mean you just don't make promises to yourself. Instead, it means when you do, you keep them. And that means you hold yourself accountable, are reliable, make achievable promises, and follow through.

Your intimate partner must also understand the importance of the same reliability and consistency and behave in that way as well. Our life partners, ideally, are our best support system. When we're taking on a new challenge, it's important to have their support. An intimate partner might be a spouse or a spouse-equivalent, or might be a trusted friend or a sibling. The role played defines the person as our intimate connection. Therefore, it's really important to share our challenges with that person and ask for the support we need.

The consequences for bad choices also need to be consistent. Everyone makes a bad choice at one time or another. Little people often make more problematic choices because that's how they learn how to make good choices. Appropriate consequences reinforce that learning. The problem with inconsistent parents is that the punishment rarely fits the crime, or consequences are applied inconsistently or inappropriately across siblings.

Compounding the problem is the use of meaningless threats. "If you do that again, Jimmy, I'll ground you until you're thirty-five." Mom knows that's not true, Jimmy knows that's not true, Jimmy's siblings know that's not true. So Jimmy does it again to see what happens. Mom makes another meaningless threat, and Jimmy gets the message there are no consequences. Then Susie accidentally spills a glass of Kool-Aid in the kitchen, and Mom, frustrated with Jimmy, grounds her for a month, which lasts three days. The message is clear: There are no meaningful consequences. That message leads to an adult who expects there will be no consequences for bad choices, which leads to more bad choices.

Consistent consequences are critical not only to the parent-child relationship but in all relationships. If you are the child of inconsistent parents, you will need to learn to impose consequences on yourself. It can be as linear as, "If I impulse-buy an outfit out of my budget, I need to return it," or "I promised myself I wouldn't drink alone, and because I did, I can't trust myself with alcohol in the house, so I'll box it all up and ask Julie to hold it for me until I feel safe with it in the house." And then stick to your self-imposed consequence.

If you're dealing with an inconsistent parent, it's important to keep your boundaries tight. You set the goals and the rules for contact. "Dad, I am so happy the kids and I will see you tomorrow. I will really appreciate it if we can have a nonpolitical visit. I know how passionate you are about your beliefs and I really honor your commitments. The kids aren't ready for politics just yet and they really love their grandfather's Lego castles."

You don't have to be rude about it, and you can be both courteous and firm.

And you can use the Sandwich Principle for delivering criticism.

The Sandwich Principle

We all know people—ourselves included—who don't like to hear criticism. Anyone who has even the slightest bit of low self-esteem hears criticism as an expression of their lack of value.

To keep your listener listening, sandwich criticism between two affirmative statements.

"Marta, you are such a wonderful cook. Tonight's dish seemed a little salty. Can you explain the recipe to me? I hope someday to be even a little bit as talented a chef as you are all the time."

"Jerry, you can really hit a baseball. Your swing is a thing of beauty. I'm concerned you aren't as interested in fielding. We really need your golden bat *and* glove in the lineup."

It's not "weasel language." It's a way to deliver a criticism with respect and kindness while still making your point. I promise that people will respond better than they do when you offer the criticism without the affirmations.

The Sandwich Principle is an excellent tool, useful not only with inconsistent parents but with anyone. People hear criticism better when you surround it with affirming statements.

We've all heard, "If you can't say something nice, don't say anything at all." In some social situations where there is little or no impact, that may be a good plan. But if you're in a relationship with someone—friend, coworker, intimate partner, parent, child, loving relative—and the person is doing something that has potential to damage your relationship or that person's with others, this person needs to hear your observation. Using the Sandwich Principle allows you to offer supportive criticism and allows them to hear you without feeling attacked and can open a dialog.

Like all tools, the Sandwich Principle requires practice and thinking.

If you were the child of inconsistent parents, you may very well have felt unpredictability was perfectly normal behavior for parents and even have taken advantage of their inconsistency to manipulate them into something you wanted. Unfortunately, most people don't like to be manipulated, as you may have discovered in your later adult relationships. Like all maladaptive tools, manipulation is a form of abuse. If you think about the emotional locations, you'll note that all the dysfunctional spots include manipulation, while the Solver spot does not. Clearly asking for what you want or need is a far better approach than manipulating another person.

It's important to recognize that virtually everybody has inconsistent moments. You're tired or down with a cold, or distracted and you "give in." That's normal human behavior. Inconsistency becomes a problem when it's your default behavior. It's then a result of reacting—just doing something in the moment because it's there—rather than responding—doing something after thinking it through and deciding on the best possible response. If you recognize you're a child of inconsistent parenting and you don't want to follow that path with your own kids, it's important for you to carefully monitor your behavior. Practice *responding with thought rather than reacting in the moment* and taking the line of least resistance.

Use clear emotional language. If your emotions and their expression are clear, the people around you will find it easier to trust what you say. That behavior also makes deposits into the trust account, an important step. Good, clear communication is critical to being consistent. When you are able to clearly say what you feel, what you need, and what you want, and then listen to the other person and come to a compromise, you're doing it right.

Be predictable, reliable, truthful, and honest.

Don't casually throw out wishful ideas. Your kids will think those are promises. If you make a promise you cannot keep, sit down with your children and, in terms they can understand, explain not only why the original plan cannot happen but also what will happen instead. If you and your co-parent are not together, it is critical that both of you live up to what you say you will do or clearly explain why it won't be possible. Your child/children have been through a lot of disruption and have trust issues to begin with. Earn their trust consistently.

Be sure the consequence fits the crime. Consistently. Across the board. And enforce what you decide. If you say a child is grounded for a week, be sure you are prepared to be grounded as well. If you are not together with a coparent who might be involved, be certain the coparent is willing and able to enforce the grounding as well. In Chapter 21, you'll find an explanation of a consequence called *focused grounding* that can help solve the grounding problem. There's an old saying that perfectly sums this up: "Don't let your mouth write a check your body won't cash."

 ## QUIZ: Am I the child of inconsistent parents?

T   F   1. The rules in our house meant something.

T   F   2. My siblings had the same rules as I did.

T   F   3. I knew what consequences there would be for certain violations.

T   F   4. If my parents promised something, it happened.

T   F   5. My parents did not threaten consequences they would not enforce.

T   F   6. I trusted my parents.

T   F   7. I know my parents trusted me.

T   F   8. I trust my intimate partner.

T   F   9. I trust myself.

Obviously, the more True answers you choose, the more consistent the parenting you experienced. If you answered False to any of the questions, you might want to look a bit deeper into your own consistency.

5

Just Not Good Enough

No matter what you do, when you do it, how you do it, or why you do it, it will never be good enough to meet unspoken expectations. Your efforts will be greeted with a sigh or an expression that says, "I'm so disappointed." Verbally it sounds like, "Well, honey, you tried," or the snottier version, "I'm sure you tried [sigh]." Sometimes it's not that affirming. Or direct.

The eternal message is, if you're perfect, I might love you. Except they won't tell you what constitutes perfect, and the "might" is the important word in the sentence because it implies the unspoken but definitely present "might not."

We all grew up with parental/family expectations of conduct and achievement. The family rules were made clear, sometimes after we had broken them, and consequences for failure were meted out. That is not the case with Just Not Good Enough (JNGE) parents. Rather than clear expectations and reasonable rules, the pressure was on to meet some unexpressed, unfocused, and unclear targets. And those targets were impossible to hit because they kept moving. Often the targets were made more unclear by being mixed with spoken expectations that might be unachievable or so low as to be insulting.

Rather than clear rewards and consequences, your efforts were met with rolled eyes and deep sighs, with condescension ("Oh, that was your best?"), with "disappointment" over and over, but never with praise or approval.

These JNGE parents pit their kids against one another in a competition to be perfect enough to be loved unconditionally. "Your brother is such a talented athlete. I'm sorry you weren't so gifted." "Your sister is so lovely and graceful," followed by a look of disappointment. Then, in a mystifying turn, these same parents will brag endlessly to their friends about you: your achievements, successes, accomplishments, and talents. The affirmations, unfortunately, will never be delivered directly to you.

Your self-esteem takes hits, repeatedly and often. And eventually it drops to the very bottom and you start to believe you're a disappointment and a failure. And all that translates to "I'm not lovable."

Not feeling loved for whom you are rather than for what you do is toxic to the soul, and the consequences can be lifelong. Not feeling loved or lovable can lead to rotten relationships that just reinforce the parental message, jobs where you don't stand up to abusive bosses, anger, depression, drug abuse, self-abuse. Or you can become an overachiever, striving to prove you are lovable and deserve love, trying to earn the respect of someone who will never give you what you need. In either case, your motivation is not healthy or positive. The reward for what you do should be feeling good about whom you are.

If you are the child of a Just Not Good Enough parent, the most important thing you can do for yourself is to change the internal message you have been delivering on their behalf. You do that by developing an internal locus of control.

LOCUS OF CONTROL

Locus of control is a concept in psychology that reflects how you gather information about yourself and your decisions and how you use that information.

Internal locus of control is a product of maturity and confidence. It's the ability to use your own internal consulting system to make your decisions. It doesn't mean you don't ask for external input; we all do. What it means is that the outside opinions do not make the final decision. You use them as advisory to your own process, not a definition of whom you are.

External locus of control is when you consult external references about most or all decisions: your social group, the clerk at the store, passersby. "How does this color work on me?" "Do you like my new haircut?" "Do you think these will taste good?" You are gathering opinions of others who may or may not know you and using them to make your decision.

If the response you get is "That puce and chartreuse houndstooth is perfect on you," and you allow that to make your decision even though you're not really feeling it's right for you, that's letting an external source make your life decisions—an external locus of control. You can see how it pairs with not feeling lovable. If you don't feel lovable, you tend to want to please others by putting their opinions ahead of yours to try to "earn" their love. That can lead you to wearing a puce and chartreuse houndstooth suit to an important meeting.

There are places where external locus is appropriate, by the way: when you ask an expert for input. At that point you are soliciting the input from someone who can give you informed, knowledgeable feedback to help you make a decision. You ask your doctor about a strange pain—totally appropriate. Asking the doctor about solutions for the pain—totally appropriate. Forcing the doctor to make your decision about care options—unhealthy external locus.

External locus of control is common among kids and teens and reflects their intense need for acceptance. It's why many adolescents express their individuality by all looking and acting exactly alike. Green hair, black nail polish, sagging pants, and a deep attachment to the favorite fashion store of the moment are all a completely normal rite of passage to the late teens and early twenties when they leave the pack and become their own persons.

Unfortunately, a young man or woman with a strong need to be loved and feel lovable will sometimes choose affiliations who do not operate in their best interests. This is fundamental to street gangs' recruitment, for example. It also opens the door to drugs, underage drinking, and high-risk behaviors, physically and socially. Anything to be accepted.

Sadly, some people do not mature out of an external locus of control and rely on the judgment and opinion of others to make their own life decisions as adults, insecure about their abilities to do anything right. Remember, others don't have the same stake in the game as you do. They are able to toss out random ideas because they have nothing to lose. You, on the other hand, are making life decisions based on casual input from people who are probably not integral to your life.

How do you develop an internal locus of control? You start by taking the risk of making a decision on your own. You can still ask others for input, but you make the final call. That puce and chartreuse houndstooth outfit? Don't buy it unless *you* love it and think you look great in it. You don't have to earn the love or admiration of the salesperson. You have to be happy. It takes time and experimentation and you will make a few clunkers of decisions, but remember everyone makes a bad decision now and then. It doesn't make them unlovable.

 ## Internal or External Locus of Control: A Quiz

T   F   1. When I'm invited to a party, I always ask what others who are going are wearing and then try to match them exactly.

T   F   2. If I'm having someone over for dinner, I always ask if they're allergic to anything so that I can avoid those foods.

T   F   3. I like to shop with my friends so that they can tell me how I look in outfits.

T   F   4. I prefer to shop alone or with a trusted friend who may or may not offer an opinion about an outfit.

T   F   5. I plan our family vacations with other members of our friends or families so we can all be together.

T   F   6. When we're going out for dinner with friends, we consult in advance about the restaurant and time.

T   F   7. I like to go to movies my friends want to see even though I might not be interested.

T   F   8. I love to read and often like authors nobody in my group of friends read.

T   F   9. I often find myself explaining my decisions to friends and family.

T   F   10. I have several groups of friends who don't overlap and I am comfortable with all of them.

If you selected the T for a majority of odd-numbered questions, you have an external locus of control. If you selected T for a majority of even-numbered questions, you have an internal locus of control. Some of these questions deserve some thought if you chose them. A balance of internal and external locus makes you pretty human.

Translating internal locus of control to dealing with an emotionally unavailable parent means you stop letting them dictate—directly or indirectly—how you feel about yourself. You confront that old refrain in your head that says nothing you have ever done or ever will do is good enough by telling yourself their beliefs are only another opinion and not your final truth. It won't happen instantly, but every time you refuse to not be good enough, you shut that refrain down a little more. Every time you make a decision for yourself without soliciting their input—or making it your sole input—you are practicing internal locus of control and building your confidence and self-esteem.

You don't have to confront your Just Not Good Enough parents. In general, they don't know they've done anything harmful or hurtful. Instead, your task is to grow beyond them; to give yourself the affirmations they weren't able to give you; to rise above your old, dysfunctional belief that you're not good enough. Your task is to see their love past the veil of expectations or to recognize they gave you all the love they could manage to give in the only form they knew. Don't start with the expectation they somehow did what they did from malice but rather from their own training or ignorance. You'll know you've succeeded when you can hear the "I love you if . . ." message and ignore the conditional.

Judy is one of those people who has so much fear about being wrong or "not good enough" she considers even constructive suggestions to be a personal attack. Her response is to get very defensive and then retreat and pout. Judy, however, is never reluctant to share her opinions and observations about others, usually without any filter or forethought. She came to my office after a major family battle that she began with her bluntness, resulting in police eventually being called and nobody in the family speaking to her.

Judy's oldest son, Jade, was especially furious with her. She had insisted it was her right to tell him how to raise his son and told him directly she didn't trust him to be alone with the little boy. Jade's former wife, Susan, had primary custody of the boy, and she and Jade had been able to work out a visitation/parenting time plan but Judy demanded to be involved. Jade lives about 1,500 miles from his son, so Judy, without consulting Jade or Susan, bought airline tickets for herself and their son and planned to stay and "watch over" the little boy while he was with Jade.

In a meeting over Skype with Judy in my office and Jade in his home, Jade pointed out angrily that Judy had been an inconsistent mother at best when he was young, sometimes hovering, other times ignoring him. He said, "I knew early on I was never going to be good enough to earn your love. I knew you thought I was just like Dad, and you made it clear you hated Dad." He paused and glared at her, then went on to say, "So now you want to tell me how to parent my kid?"

Judy became enraged and paced around my office, glowering and shutdown, so I put up a time-out signal and said, "Just a minute. We're not getting where we need to go here." I asked both of them to take a ten-minute break to calm down.

Judy paced angrily for a few minutes, then burst into tears. "He's right. I did hate Richard, Jade's dad. And Jade looked just like him. I didn't hate Jade, I love him and I wanted him to be better than his dad, so I did what my parents did: I didn't praise him because I didn't want him to get a fat head."

Jade had been listening. "I didn't get a fat head, Mom. I got a feeling I was never going to be good enough for you. No matter what I did, no matter how hard I tried, I have never been able to believe I was doing it right or well or good enough to be loved by you or anyone. So now when you say I'm not a good dad, that goes right to my heart, and I'm afraid you're right. I have to build my relationship with my boy, and to do that we have to have time alone together."

Judy was still weeping but she was able to acknowledge Jade for his truth and admit she hadn't been a perfect mom. She also made a small apology but surrounded it with defensive explanations/excuses. We worked on that in ongoing sessions, and eventually she made a genuine and sincere apology to Jade on later calls. They are still working on correcting those old messages, but Jade is spending "unsupervised" time with his son and they're doing well. Small steps.

A parent who gives a child the message that the child is not good enough is actually reflecting the parent's own profound insecurities. The parent doesn't want you to feel lovable or worthy because the parents don't feel lovable or worthy of love. Sadly, these sort of messages tend to be generational. Great-grandfather was clear with Grandmother she wasn't worthy of his love or attention because she was female. What he didn't say was that his disdain for her was rooted in his fear of his own strong mother, and Grandmother reminded him of his mother. Grandmother then overvalued her sons rather than her daughters because she had the message from Great-grandfather that women are less than.

And yet she watched her daughters succeed in their lives and was proud of them. So she bragged to her friends about how smart and successful her daughters are. And she bragged to her daughters how wonderful her sons are. That's how your mom acquired her never-be-good-enough mentality as well as her consequent feelings of insecurity. Then you came along and she used the tools she had learned in her family of origin to assess your lovability. So no matter how lovable you are, you don't get that message.

Stop the cycle! You deserve to be happy, to be loved, to be respected, to be honored, to be recognized not only for whom you are but also for what you do. You are good enough. You're more than good enough: You're the perfect you.

AFFIRMATIONS

Those positive statements are called affirmations, and they are effective when you deliver them to yourself. One way to do so is to write yourself notes and post them all over your life:

"I deserve to be loved."
"I am perfect just the way I am."
"I am good enough."
"I make good choices."
"I deserve to be happy."

Write these sorts of messages on Post-it notes and stick them where you will see them every day. Read them out loud. When you do, your brain gets the message from two different sources: visual and auditory. It reinforces the positive message.

I guarantee you will be uncomfortable the first few times you do this because those old messages in your head of not being good enough do not want to be evicted. They have been in your brain and your life for a long time and are comfortable there. Even though they make you uncomfortable, keep reading the affirmations in a firm, confident voice.

The next step is to stand in front of the mirror, look yourself in the eye, and confidently recite your affirmations. Say it loud, say it proud: "I am good enough." "I deserve to be happy." "I deserve to be loved." This is a big step, and those old messages might fight your resolve with vigor. Don't give up. If the first time you do this your voice sounds like a whisper, or you laugh or even cry, you are still delivering the message. And the next time you do it, you'll do better. Because you are good enough and you do deserve to be loved. Especially by you!

Sandra is a tall, willowy, blonde woman in her late thirties. She's a researcher at a university and has a PhD. She arrived in my office for our first meeting wearing baggy khakis, a black T-shirt, and a cardigan sweater. She wasn't wearing any makeup. She spoke barely above a whisper.

"My mom is difficult," she said, apologetically. "I'm sure it's because we don't really match very well. I don't have much in common with her. She doesn't really like anything I like, but I'm sure it's probably because I don't try hard enough to like what she likes." She stared at the floor.

I asked her to tell me what she liked. "Well, I like to read and I like my job, but what I really love is old movies." For the first time she smiled. "Busby Berkeley and the great films of the thirties and forties just carry me away. I think I must have lived another life at that time in history."

Mom, on the other hand, was into yoga, meditation, communes, and philosophy. She loved to travel, but her destinations were always retreats of one kind or another, which Sandra described as "buggy, uncomfortable, raw food, hepatitis breeding grounds." Her voice had gotten small again. "I tried to go with her to one in Guatemala. I tried all the exercises and the food and the sleeping in hammocks and the chanting and hated every minute of it. And that was before I got dysentery. Mom told me my attitude had opened the door to the dysentery because of my negative energy. Maybe she was right because nobody else got sick. I've always been a disappointment to her."

As we worked together I kept pushing her to talk about her achievements and accomplishments even though she felt uncomfortable. At first, every positive statement was offset by a criticism, clearly an implanted message from her mom. Although she wouldn't say so, I know she was irritated with me when I would interrupt her criticism to ask whose voice she was hearing in her head. Sandra caught on quickly to my questions and began interrupting herself.

The next step was for her to confront the criticisms with the reality of her life, and as she did, her confidence in herself began to grow. She sat up straighter, met my eyes, and her voice strengthened.

After several months of weekly sessions, Sandra arrived at my office with a new energy. She had begun wearing makeup and her hair was carefully groomed. A chic outfit had replaced the khakis and cardigan, and she was smiling. "I have an idea. I think I'm ready to let my mom know I am who I am and I don't have to be her to be lovable."

It was time for the three-sentence rule. A quick reminder:

When you are having an emotional discussion,
limit yourself to three sentences, then stop
and let the other party respond.

The three-sentence rule isn't as easy to follow as it might sound. You're all full of emotional energy, and you want to say everything you have to say as quickly as possible. Unfortunately, what you're trying to convey often comes out in a jumble, and the other party is busy thinking of how to respond—or react—rather than listening to your point.

When you have to limit yourself to three sentences, you think more about what you want to say and the other party can listen to your point. Sandra and I practiced the three-sentence rule for a couple of sessions before she invited her mom to join us for a session.

Sandra's mom surprised me. I had expected an older version of Sandra, but she was of average height and had dark, curly hair. Their smiles and shapes of their faces marked them as mother and daughter.

"Barbara," she announced with a big smile, shaking my hand, "I'm here to do anything I can for my brilliant daughter. Isn't she beautiful? And smart. I am so lucky. I just couldn't be more proud of her."

Sandra's skeptical eyebrow raise caught my eye.

Barbara tried to control the session by asking about my background, the art in my office, and other trivia. I let her talk for a few minutes, getting comfortable, then led the conversation to Sandra.

"Mom, you and I don't have a lot in common."

"Well, if you were willing to give things a real try—"

Sandra held up her hand in a stop gesture, and Barbara, apparently stunned, stopped talking.

"As I was saying, we don't have a lot in common. That doesn't need to make us either distant from each other or enemies. I respect your devotion to your spiritual life." Then she stopped.

Barbara looked surprised. "I thought you hated it."

"I don't hate it for you; I hate it for me. I prefer my old movies and my books. And lately I've begun swimming again."

"Are you taking vitamins? You know vitamins are the key to real health. You just don't get enough nutrition from food, even if it's organic. You remember Jim? You met him in Guatemala although your attitude—" Barbara tried to take control, but Sandra was able to stop her again.

"Mom, we don't have to be the same or like the same things to love and respect each other. I respect your choices, though I don't share them. I would like to feel respected by you."

Barbara opened her mouth to reply, made a gesture with her hand, then nodded. "That . . . seems . . . reasonable. I had never thought of it that way. Of course I respect you. I brag to my friends about you all the time. They tease me about it." She stopped talking and shook her head.

Sandra looked directly into Barbara's eyes. "The problem is you never brag to me about me."

Tears slid from Barbara's eyes. In a very small voice she said, "I'm so sorry. Thank you for telling me. I'll work on it."

The last time I saw Sandra, they were both working on it.

Not everyone who confronts a Just Not Good Enough parent gets Sandra's outcome. Often, unfortunately, a confrontation makes critics more critical as they defend their position. If you feel strong enough and can find the right time and the right words—gentle but firm—asking to be respected and treated with kindness is empowering and appropriate. You might feel scared or intimidated, but before you give up, ask yourself what you have to lose. Then ask yourself what you have to gain.

To quote the Great One, Wayne Gretzky, "One hundred percent of shots not taken do not go in the net."

6

In His or
Her Own Reality

Carlton is a really nice man. His wife of thirty-six years adores him. His two sons and one daughter are all happily married. They shook their heads with loving amusement when I asked them to tell me about him since he had brought everyone to our first session.

"Dad's an interesting guy. He reads a lot. He likes roller coasters and college basketball and he's a great dad. He's a really good computer whiz and loves his job." Chad, the oldest son, elicited nods from the rest of the family, including Carlton.

"Thanks, Son. Those are nice words, and I appreciate them."

We spent the rest of the session talking about family history, and Carlton agreed to come back to address his issues with his brother's death. About the first thirty minutes of our second session focused on exactly that topic.

"You know," Carlton suddenly said to me conspiratorially, "it's entirely possible this is all being recorded."

I held my hands up, open. "Not by me. I don't record sessions without written consent by the client."

He nodded. "Not by either of us. Have you had your office swept?"

I was completely puzzled. He had come in to process the death of his brother from cancer. At least that's what he'd told me. He worked as a computer engineer for a school system and had lived his whole life in his community.

"Swept?"

"For bugs. You never know."

"Carlton, who might be bugging my office? And why?"

He wandered around the office, picking up pillows and looking behind books and pictures. "I'm not accusing anyone, mind you," he said, more loudly than normal conversation, inspecting the back of a framed print. "Just pointing out everyone is," he dropped to his knees, running his hands along the bottom of the love seat, "vulnerable to," looking under the coffee table, "surveillance." He finished his inspection. "Let me check your desk."

I figured we weren't going to get anywhere unless I agreed, so I stepped out of the way and he checked the drawers and underside before he was satisfied and returned to the chair.

"You might be clear," he said, eyeing the air-conditioner vent.

"Carlton, I thought we were here to talk about your brother's sad passing. Is there something more?"

"You can't be too careful," he said, enigmatically. "One thing often leads to another."

My mentor once told me, "Be with the client where they are," so I decided to follow his rather unusual path to where it might be going.

"Let's go back for a minute to why you are concerned about my office being bugged. Help me understand your concerns."

He sighed, pursed his lips, gave another glance to the vent, then said, "It's very complicated. I've been doing research about it on the Internet for a long time, and it's really multilayered. Not to take up the rest of our time, but let's just say it has to do with the occult world government." He went on to explain about a secret organization formed by an offshoot of the United Nations that had various missions, mostly involving population reduction and development of an alien-welcoming environment. Aliens from another planet. He never did get down to why my office might be part of the operation.

"Tell me about your work," I finally managed to interject.

Carlton then described his job, his family, and his relationships in lucid and non paranoid terms, expressing emotions clearly and without any lack of reality. He was able to talk about his brother's death, with appropriate tears and smiles at the memories of their good times together. There was no further foray into the occult world government. Over time this was consistent.

During the time Carlton and I met, his second-oldest son, Erik, asked to come in on his own. "I suppose you've heard about the occult world government by now," he said.

I nodded.

"Look, my dad isn't crazy, but my brother and sister and I worry about him. Just when we think he's gotten past it, it all flares up again. The last flare-up was the day before my sister's wedding. He tore the church apart looking for bugs. Mom lost it, Susan lost it. The wedding almost didn't happen. Then he was fine on her big day, but we were all a wreck. He doesn't seem to realize what it does to the family. It's just really hard to trust him. He ended up not coming to my college graduation because he was convinced the 'invasion' was imminent."

Of course, everyone has the right to believe what they believe. And, in general, a belief system is not toxic. However, when immersion in a belief system begins to get in the way of regular life and relationships, it becomes a problem.

Carlton and others like him are not schizophrenic or psychotic. They function well in much of their lives. Rather they get attached to an idea or a belief system and then do research and reading that bolsters their belief or idea, reinforcing it while ignoring conflicting information and scientific evidence. Once that attachment forms, it's almost impossible to introduce any conflicting information, fact, or opinion.

Cognitive Dissonance

Sometimes people hold a core belief that is very strong.

When they are presented with evidence that works against that belief, the new evidence cannot be accepted.

It would create a feeling that is extremely uncomfortable called cognitive dissonance.

And because it is so important to protect the core belief, they will rationalize, ignore, and even deny anything that doesn't fit in with the core belief.

—Frantz Fanon

This sort of attachment to an idea goes beyond conspiracy theories to politics, religion, medical issues and treatment, finances, child rearing, education, and a myriad of other human activities. The difficulties arise when you are at odds with their core belief and then become more complex when you are dealing with your parents who expect your loyalty and see disagreement as rejection.

As people get into their elder years, eccentricities can become full-on personality disorders (more about those later), just as the perfectly normal stage arrives in which their social veneer can fall away. The "old guy" in the neighborhood who waves his fist and yells at the kids crossing his yard probably wouldn't have done that same thing fifteen years before. He began when he starting losing his social veneer—the face we all agree to present to the public world—and, as a consequence, gave himself permission to begin yelling at kids. He probably also yells at his relatives. And argues with the TV. And holds in high contempt a lot of cultural changes from "my day."

If you are his son or daughter, you're confronted with the loss of the parent you knew and loved and the emergence of this angry, stubborn, disdainful person. So how to confront core beliefs and behavior that are making your relationship strained and difficult? One step at a time.

First, recognize you can't argue them out of the idea or behavior. They are where they are; they believe what they believe. If you disagree, state your disagreement clearly and respectfully without the expectation of acceptance.

"Mom, you and I don't share the same political views. I hope you understand I love you. Can we just not discuss politics?" And then stick to it.

"Dad, I've been thinking about what fun my friends and I had playing in the yard with you when I was little. It's a shame the kids in your neighborhood haven't had the opportunity to get to know you like that."

It may require many repetitions and much encouragement and, depending upon the parent, may not be successful, but it doesn't mean you shouldn't try.

Second, you need to set firm boundaries about what you and your family will tolerate. "Dad, I understand you believe the occult world government is trying to drug people with fluoride and chemtrails. Respectfully, I ask you not to share your beliefs around my kids. It scares them, and I don't want them to be afraid of Grandpa." Then stick to your guns.

Third, you need to follow through with consequences for breaches of those boundaries. "Dad, I've asked you a couple of times not to talk about fluoride and chemtrails around the kids, and you've disrespected my boundaries. The kids will be taking two weeks away from you, and I hope that will reinforce that I don't want the kids to be scared of or by you." You don't have to be rude or angry when setting boundaries, just clear and firm. And willing to back up what you say with action.

What's the line between eccentric and needs help? If you think back to the standards I used with Carlton, you'll begin to get a picture. Carlton functioned just fine in the world: job, family, friends, social life. He just had attached himself to a belief that sometimes got in his way. Without the occult world government, he was well within the bell curve of normal.

Hallucinations—hearing voices or seeing things others cannot see; delusions—thinking the FBI or CIA is listening to thoughts through dental work, for example; self-harming behavior—cutting or burning or suicide attempts; paralyzing depression or hypermanic energy would all be reasons to seek input from a physician. Your primary consideration is the safety of the person and the community around them.

It's a difficult process to watch someone you love change into someone cantankerous and moody. Don't overanalyze your parents, but also avoid the trap of denial. Carlton's beliefs may not be mainstream, but they are also not mental illness–style delusions. They're his beliefs, and he is entitled to them. He has done a lot of reading that supports his beliefs, which has reinforced his position. He's been talking about his theories and researching them over a long period of time without having any impact on his behavior in the rest of his life, except perhaps boring his family.

Someone who is experiencing dementia or Alzheimer's or a mental decline will express much more random, disorganized thoughts. There won't be research to bolster their beliefs because they will not have organized form. People who have the beginning symptoms of Alzheimer's or dementia know strange things are going on in their minds. They forget things, put belongings in odd places, and experience confusion about dates and times, but there are also many times when they are fully aware and can recall the problem moments. You can imagine how scary this must be.

There are medications that address some of these symptoms, and your family physician or a gerontologist—a medical specialty focused on elders— should be involved as soon as symptoms appear. Sometimes your persuasion skills will be tested to get your affected parent to participate because it's hard to acknowledge and accept something that changes your life.

Don't nag. Don't beg. Make the appointment and go along. Take notes, ask questions, be supportive.

Most of all, don't panic. There are answers, and you are not alone.

7

Hovering Controllers

Dance moms. Pageant parents. Terrorizers of teachers, coaches, school administrators, medical professionals, and their own children. They have a firm grip on every aspect of their children's lives and are always ready to do battle with anyone who presumes not to acknowledge their total dominance in every situation involving their child.

The child of a hovering controller never needs to make decisions—they are made by the parent. This is necessary when the child is two months old, problematic at twelve, totally inappropriate after twenty. One of the great gifts a parent can give a child is the ability to make good decisions. If children never have the opportunity to test their decision-making skills, they will make the same mistakes again and again, particularly if the hovering controller parent rushes in to "save" them from their consequences.

It's not just about decision making. The hovering controller also has virtually nonexistent boundaries so doesn't see the line between themselves and their children. Instead, they tend to absorb their children's lives, ultimately erasing any differentiation. And that's important because one of the jobs of parenting is to encourage the child to become his or her own person, called *individuation*.

Successful adults know who they are. They also know who others are and where the line exists between the two. That's having boundaries. Having boundaries enables a person to be an individual, and that process begins in early childhood in small steps. At about eighteen months, a parent offers the child the choice between an apple and a pear. The baby makes a choice. This is the beginning of individuation. There is no bad choice between the two, but choice itself represents power, and the ability to trust oneself evolves from knowing how to manage that power.

At age three or four, kids start to become aware that not everyone lives the same way they do. Up until that time they are developing enough language and memory to be able to store the lives of their families and trying to figure out their extended family. It may be preschool or church or a play group, but there will come a moment when Jordan realizes his buddy Brett doesn't have a daddy living in the house or Amanda hears her friend Maria speaking another language. Suddenly Jordan and Amanda see their lives are different from those of their friends, and most important, different is okay. This is individuation on a couple of levels: I am different from you and my family is different from your family, and it's fine.

Throughout childhood this awareness of differences helps kids progress toward the individuation of adulthood. Individuation gets pretty intense in adolescence. During this time kids are trying to figure out who they are by watching and imitating their peers. Parents and family still have influence, but much less than the cadre of friends. Making it worse, adolescence is also a know-it-all time during which the teen individuates, in part, by arguing with or defying parental authority. As infuriating as it is, it's a really important step to becoming one's own person. Or as my own mother so succinctly put it, "You can cut the apron strings, but don't stab me in the back with the scissors."

The hovering controller short-circuits the individuation process by taking away the child's power of choice. Rather than letting their child take a risk or make a mistake, they intervene, making decisions without consulting or including the child.

"Tony will play baseball this year. He wanted to try lacrosse, but I don't like lacrosse so he's playing baseball. He's good at baseball. And I'm going to volunteer to help the coach." Tony will have Dad not only making the decision about what game he'll play but also have Dad on the bench,

second-guessing the coach and "rescuing" Tony from any potential humiliation or disappointment. And everyone will get a trophy because other hovering controller parents are on the community athletic association board
and want to protect their children from disappointment.

Teaching a kid how to handle disappointment is critical to individuation. Life does not hand out trophies for showing up. There are winners and
losers in every activity of the adult world, and the person who encounters
disappointment without the tools to handle it is at a huge disadvantage.
Learning to manage disappointment begins with being able to hear "no"
and accept it as an outcome. We've all been in Target when some frazzled
parent is being harangued by a screaming toddler who wants something
the parent is unwilling to buy. This is tantrum-based negotiation and the
perfect opportunity to teach an important truth:

No is a complete sentence.

It's really important not to give in to tantrum-based negotiation—with
a toddler or with an adult—because not only are you not teaching how to
manage disappointment but you are also teaching them what it takes to
break your will. Once that lesson comes home, your battle is lost.

Hovering controllers say no but don't take the time to teach; instead they
just take away control and choice. The child submits, losing personal power.

SURRENDER is the ability to choose
to allow someone else to be in control;
SUBMISSION is having control forced upon you.

When you board an airplane or a bus or a cruise ship, you are choosing
to trust the expertise of the person at the controls. You glance at the pilot
as you board the plane to reassure yourself she seems to be competent

and alert and then you sit in your seat and buckle up. You could choose to get off the plane before takeoff. You also know the pilot is assisted—and watched—by the copilot. Both of them are accountable to the airline as well as the FAA. You make the choice to let them have control while you are on the plane. You voluntarily *surrender*.

With *submission*, your ability to choose is taken away. There is no choice. Obviously, prison is a good example of a situation in which there is submission, but hovering controllers also demand submission. No arguments, no negotiation, no choice. Without choice, you have no power. Without power, your life is not your own and you arrive at adulthood without the necessary skills to be an adult. When children of hovering controllers become adults, they lack the ability to make their own decisions and either completely run amok or are unable to do anything in their lives without their parents making the decisions for them.

"You should marry Byron. He'll be successful."

"But I don't love Byron." In a very small, quiet voice.

"I didn't ask if you love Byron. I said you should marry him. Now let's plan your wedding."

At work, they defer to the person who exhibits the most control—often the office bully—and are isolated from people who might support their efforts to become their own person. Instead, they choose another hovering controller and do as they are told. They are uncomfortably comfortable with letting someone else make their decisions for them.

This is the principle that creates street gangs, motorcycle gangs, and cults: a charismatic leader who exercises total control over subordinates, demands absolute loyalty, emphasizes "we are different from others, therefore better," and expects no opposition from anyone. Certainly not all children of hovering controllers become gang members or join cults, but an inordinate number of members of gangs and cults are disempowered children who have not learned to take control of their own lives.

As the hovering controller gets older, the need for control grows and efforts to maintain control over adult children increase. This make take the form of open demands—"You need to come over right now and fix my television"—or a more passive-aggressive demand—"I'm so lonely. I don't have anyone to talk to, but I know you're busy . . . [sigh]."

This can lead to the pernicious version of the hovering controller: the I-own-you parent. An I-own-you parent remembers everything ever done for you and wants you to balance the ledger. The problem is it will never be in balance because they have been keeping track not only of reality but also of imagined bequests.

"Do you remember when I paid for your class ring in high school? You never paid me back." The fact you're now fifty-three and have no recollection of where your high school class ring is or even any memory if it ever existed doesn't matter. "Well, that's water under the bridge but now I need . . . ," and then comes the demand for "repayment." The underlying message of the demand is "You owe me, so I own you."

If you fulfill the demand, there will be another and another and another. If you resist, you will find yourself either frozen out or besieged with escalating demands and reminders of all they have sacrificed for you over the course of your entire life. Both will be guilt-infested.

There is a solution. When you are reminded of a "favor" granted or a "sacrifice" made, immediately express your appreciation. Excessively. "I do remember you took a day off so we could go look at colleges, Dad, and I can't tell you how much that meant to me. You were right: Madison was the perfect place for me. I'm so glad we did that together."

Your praise and recollection of the "debt" derails the demand. Beyond that, it also honors the things the parent has done for you and reinforces the connection between you. In many cases, the loss of the parent/child connection in the "old way" is what they are missing. Every parent wants to feel as though they did the best job they could at parenting and wants acknowledgment you share their view. The I-own-you parent has converted the need for confirmation into a ledger. Once you understand the message hiding under the overt message, the ledger will begin to disappear.

In all but the most toxic parent/child relationships, there are good moments. You may have to dig deep, but doing so might give you some unexpected benefits. First, honoring the efforts at effective parenting of the

I-own-yous or hovering controllers may lessen their need to control because they will be able to embrace your acknowledgment of their actions.

Second, these acknowledgments can open the door to establishing an adult-adult relationship. Often I-own-you or hovering controller parents have been unable to let go of their role with you when you were a child, so they have behaved in a controlling way because in their minds you're still a child. Their child. Not so oddly, when we return to our parents' home, even if it's not our childhood home, we revert in many subtle ways to our child behaviors. It might be calling your parent Mommy or Daddy or it could be a re-creation of a dramatic adolescent/parent conflict that has no foundation in the present. We have to actively form adult-adult relationships with I-own-yous or hovering controllers or these child behaviors will persist. Acknowledgments of their contributions to your adult life are a place to begin.

Finally, your own self-esteem will improve. Being constantly on guard or trying to avoid contact with a controlling parent is draining. Add in a measure of guilt—and most of us are vulnerable to guilt whether we like to admit it or not—and your self-esteem drops as your stress rises. When you can set some of those burdens down and have more positive interactions with your parents, I guarantee you will feel better about yourself and about them.

8

Brainiacs:
All Think, No Feel

To the brainiac, parenting is an intellectual exercise. Actually, life is an intellectual exercise. Unfortunately, their children are also unexposed to an emotional life and so have, at minimum, confused responses to their own feelings and an inability to read the emotions of others. At worst, they can become compassionless narcissists.

Gail grew up in New Zealand in a large, expressive family. Her dad was a high-functioning alcoholic who was not reliable in terms of providing for his family but was loving and demonstrative with his wife and seven kids. Mom was the family organizer who kept everything running smoothly. Gail defined her as "practical and efficient, but with a good sense of humor. She wasn't very emotional but she didn't really have the time. Seven kids over ten years took a lot of the emotions away. And Pop was always hugging on us. He was emotional enough for both of them."

Gail met Jack when she was on vacation with girlfriends in Bali. Jack was in the U.S. Army, stationed in Korea, and on leave. They had a whirlwind weeklong romance. She liked that he didn't drink and seemed rock solid. He was proud of his military service, and she respected that as well. They emailed back and forth and met again six months later in New Zealand. He met her parents then and proposed. He returned to Korea, they continued emailing, and just before he was to return to the United States three months later, they were married in a small courthouse ceremony with her family attending.

"I packed everything I owned into two suitcases and moved to the States," she told me at our first meeting. "Married to a guy I barely knew. Of course I thought I knew him. But I was twenty. What did I know about anything?"

Jack's family, she discovered, was unemotional, distant, and formal. She stayed with them for three months while Jack concluded his army commitment, then they moved to Atlanta where his new job required more than 50 percent travel.

"I was alone in a city where I didn't know anyone, in a country where I didn't know anyone. I tried to talk to my mother-in-law, and she was full of advice but didn't talk about feelings at all. I wanted support, and what I got were suggestions, one of which was that I needed to stop being emotional. I did take one of her suggestions and got a job, and that's where I met some friends and started to find a support system. When Jack was home we were so busy we rarely spent time just alone and getting to really know one another."

Jack eventually got promoted and his travel schedule was reduced, so they began to spend more time together.

"I'd been married to Jack for almost four years, but we'd actually spent a total of less than a year together. It was when he was home more I finally figured out he had no emotions. None. He doesn't feel anything. He's like a monotone hum emotionally. And I feel everything. And now here we are: married almost twenty years with two daughters and he never shows any emotions still. When his dad died, the family gathered and it was a business meeting, not a funeral. The girls and I cried. Jack and his family looked embarrassed. My mother-in-law kept telling me to get a hold of myself."

When Jack joined us, Gail's assessment turned out to be true. Jack's face was a mask that never changed, no matter what we talked about. I brought up his daughters' births and his father's death to see if there were any different reactions to two very opposite emotional situations. He nodded and said, "Emotional. Both were very emotional." But his face never changed nor did his body language.

I asked, "Can you put a name to any of those emotions?"

He shrugged. "Of course." But he couldn't.

Gail, meanwhile, was in tears. "That's my whole point, Jack. You never learned emotions."

Jack shrugged again. "I don't know why that's a bad thing. I'm very logical and I make a lot of money and we have a nice life. We have two beautiful girls. Why does it matter?" Even though his words were emotional, his face and body language remained impassive.

We worked together for several months, but Jack's position on emotions never changed. Gail continued to ask for what she needed, and he continued to stonewall her. His formal, distant, unemotional family had taught him emotions were unnecessary, and he couldn't see any reason to change. Sadly, they stopped coming to therapy.

The difference between intellect and feelings is enormous. We all need both. The practical, problem-solving parts of life need intellectual application and clear decision making: *operational* functions. Relationships require the expression of feelings: *emotional* functions.

Jack is all operational and probably feels unsafe or uncomfortable when he encounters emotions in others or himself, though he doesn't permit himself to feel or express them. The truth is that everyone has feelings, even Jack. It comes down to a willingness to experience them. Jack and other children of brainiac parents have not been taught how to manage or experience their emotional lives, so they choose to ignore or suppress what they feel, staying in their heads.

Gail learned emotions from her dad and, to some degree, her mom. She learned the balance between emotional and operational.

Brainiacs are detached from their emotions because they're stuck in their heads. What their kids most want is that emotional connection with their parents, but brainiacs don't make the link, instead staying intellectual and pushing emotions to the back. When these kids grow up to be adults, they are wary of emotions, again because they can't trust their own emotions.

As brainiac parents age and the social veneer starts to erode, they may surprise their emotionally restricted children by expressing a wide range of feelings, some appropriate, some inappropriate since they are not experienced in feelings. This can be a result of their need to relax control as they move into retirement or, sadly, a result of a form of dementia. In either case, their emotion-restricted children suddenly have to develop a new foundation for the relationship, creating confusion all around.

Jack is a really extreme version of an operational person, but he is not alone. If you recognize your family or yourself as being operational or out of balance leaning toward operational and away from emotional, it's important to you and your relationships not to retreat from feelings like Jack did, but rather to work with a therapist who can help you learn to express your own feelings and recognize feelings in others. It's not an overnight process and you might very well be uncomfortable while you're working on it, but the work will pay off in more balanced, more connected, more rewarding, and less confusing relationships with the people who mean the most to you.

If you are an emotional person in a relationship with a brainiac, your emotions likely will not be interpreted correctly or will be seen as excessive or overwhelming. That doesn't mean you shouldn't feel and express your emotions, but rather you need to be clear about what you feel using the basic four emotions—mad, glad, sad, and scared—and temper your expectations of how the brainiac will respond.

 ## Are You Operational or Emotional?

    T   F   1. I prefer to talk about facts when I'm with loved ones.

    T   F   2. When there is a problem to be solved, I spend time thinking about not only my feelings and ideas but also the feelings and ideas of others.

    T   F   3. I like to watch documentaries on television but I also like movies that are fictional.

T   F   4. I pay close attention to people's body language when they're speaking.

T   F   5. Sometimes the news is just too much for me and I have to turn it off.

T   F   6. I'm uncomfortable with people who are too emotional or too rigid.

T   F   7. One of my favorite things is a raucous game of cards with friends.

T   F   8. I've always been the quiet one in my family.

T   F   9. I like to listen to debates.

If you chose T on 1, 8, 9—You're more operational.
If you chose T on 4, 5, 7—You're more emotional.

Gail's mistake was to exaggerate her emotions in hope that a more vivid display would be clearer to Jack. Instead, he retreated further, creating a cycle of misunderstanding and misinterpretation between them.

Another sort of brainiac is the information-gathering brainiac parent who relies on the advice of every child-rearing "expert" encountered. Books, blogs, friends, and relatives all give input, which the parent absorbs and applies, indiscriminately, even if the advice is contradictory.

Some of these experts are truly experts: people who, through experience, education, and thought, have created a plan or approach that works. Other true experts might be parents who have done a great job with their own kids. The "experts" who aren't necessarily so are those who advocate for extremes—discipline, diet, wellness. Unfortunately, the information-gathering brainiac doesn't always discriminate between the sensible and the extreme. Information, they believe, is power, and being able to pass along information confers "power" to them. The truth is, rather, they don't trust themselves and their own "internal expert" so seek those external sources to confer "authority" to what they say and believe.

The damage to their kids comes from the confusion of the polyglot of rules and expectations that arise from following all the leaders. During their most impressionable and formative years, children inherently trust their parents, no matter whether their parents deserve to be trusted or not. Research shows that most kids' personalities are solidified by about age six, so parental inconsistencies in those early years become part of whom that child grows up to be. Following too many paths and using too many different approaches teaches children not to expect consistency and therefore not to trust their parents during the time their personalities are being formed. Unfortunately, that lack of trust continues into adulthood and can create relationship problems with spouses, partners, coworkers, and their own kids.

If you're going to rely on experts—and there is nothing wrong with listening to and following *authentic* experts—be sure you do a couple of things:

First, make sure they really are experts and have the credentials and experience to back up their expertise. You wouldn't go to a dermatologist for brain surgery. The person might be an amazing dermatologist, but that does not make her even a marginal brain surgeon. Yes, both are doctors but experts only in their own fields.

Second, choose a plan or an approach and stick with it. Don't go all over the map just because something distracts you from your plan or seems like a good idea. If it's working, don't fix it.

Finally, rely on your own instincts. You know yourself and your kids. Trust your own internal expertise.

If you are the child of an information-gathering brainiac, what you need most in your life is a plan and structure—things you didn't get with the expertise shifting constantly when you were a kid. You can create your own structure using parameters that already exist in your life. Your job schedule, regular appointments such as the gym or your therapist, school, time with friends, meals, and bedtime all contribute to your schedule, which is structure. Be consistent with yourself. Structure creates security and allows you to be able to feel and express your feelings, which will improve your relationships.

If you are dealing with an information-gathering brainiac parent, under-stand that the reliance on external experts probably arises from insecurities about his own abilities to use his own internal expert. As people age, those insecurities may get stronger and their reliance on "experts" may get stron-ger. What this can mean for you in dealing with them is more arguments, stubbornness, and distraction. They will still want their chosen experts to be the source of your choices, even if you don't agree.

It will be really important for you to use clear communication when dealing with information-gathering brainiacs because they listen not only to what you say but also to how you say it. Using "I feel" language will help you be clear that you employ feelings in your communication and expect they will at least try.

Rather than engaging in battles destined to create friction or conflict, thank them for their help and input—then do what your internal expert advises is best for you.

9

Glory Days Parents

He was the star quarterback in high school and lives to reminisce about the "big game" and his "big play" that saved it. Endlessly. Not only with his friends but also with his kids' friends. He still wears his high school letter jacket. He adopts all the new slang and wants to be accepted as "the cool dad" or even as a peer with his children's crowd, particularly when they reach their teens.

She works out every day, eats sparingly, tans, has a Botox resource, and chooses a wardrobe from Forever 21. Unfortunately, she's far from twenty-one. Low-cut, tight tops with deep cleavage; micro-mini skirts; and Daisy Duke shorts or skin-tight jeans complete her look. She wears a lot of makeup. She likes to hang out with her daughter's friends and their boyfriends but sometimes even more with her son's friends.

Obviously these two are the easy target stereotypes of Glory Days parents. There are other embodiments for sure and we'll look at some of those, but the message of all Glory Days parents is the same: I am not only your peer but also your competition.

The process of aging gracefully isn't always an easy one, and certainly some people do it better ... and worse ... than others. It's hard in our youth-obsessed culture to step away from some of the fun fashions or cool things to do aimed at late teens and twentysomethings. Magazines, media, and movies all present these age groups as being the ideal—perfect skin, youth, energy, freedom, physical power—all are very appealing. The problem arises when people in their forties or fifties try to present themselves as still part of that demographic.

Glory Days parents are desperately trying to hold onto their youth, when they felt powerful or appealing. It's almost as though they develop mirror blindness as they don't see their true reflection, instead seeing themselves as they were or, more sadly, as they hoped they were.

This is not to say a person can't reminisce about one's early life. Some of our best stories and memories come from those ages of innocence/stupidity/risk taking primarily because we learned from those experiences and grew beyond them.

Glory Days parents are emotionally stuck in those days but, instead of acknowledging the lessons they have learned, spend their time clinging to their past triumphs. Ultimately these choices mean they may miss out on the good parts of the rest of their lives, deserting the present in favor of the past.

I've heard aging athletes say, "The older I get, the faster I was." That's another problem for Glory Days parents: Memory has a way of clouding reality so that with each retelling, the events get a little distorted and a little more favorable. As a child hears the story morph over time, it makes the parent look like a liar and erodes trust.

A more pernicious Glory Days parent is one who is in direct competition with a child. This can take the form of business, sports, or relationships, and sometimes all at once.

I met Mike and his dad, George, in the midst of a family crisis. Mike had not spoken to George for six months when they first came in after finding out George was having yet another affair, this time with a woman Mike had been dating.

Mike, divorced and in his mid thirties, was furious. "This has to be at least the tenth affair he's had," speaking as though his father weren't sitting across the room. "He's cheated on my mother for the forty-three years they've been married, and he doesn't think there's anything wrong with that."

"Son, it's my life."

Mike glared daggers at his father. "It's not just your life. It's also Mom's life and Geraldine's life and my life. Particularly my life once you started . . . with Becky."

"Son, she started it. She came on to me. She told me you were controlling her and treating her like crap, which, by the way, I knew was right. She was crying, and one thing just led to another. I guess she was just attracted to my energy. She said she really likes athletes."

Mike clenched his teeth. "Don't even go there." He stood and grabbed his jacket, glared at George, then sat back down. "I can't let that stand. I'm sure you told her your usual BS sports hero stories and charmed her . . . except for a few missing details like you knew Becky and I were having trouble but you fed into her bull. And we'd been together for a long time and hung out with you and Mom. And one thing led to another for six weeks? What the hell? Why didn't you say 'no'? And did she know where I learned to be controlling?"

"Now, Son," George said placatingly, "that's a whole different subject. You know you were a handful as a kid, and I had to keep you in line. And you wouldn't play sports, so I was forced to do what I had to."

Mike snorted and turned away, then turned back to me. "Yeah, I was a busy kid. I was always in Dad's shadow, according to him. I wasn't the athlete he had been and that apparently made me undesirable as a son. So yeah, I acted out."

George interjected, "Busy? You were a criminal. And a smooth talker. You shot your friend. And got probation. You stole stuff: cars, bikes, money, damn near anything you could get your hands on. I put my energy into being a good athlete."

Mike glared at George. "And sometimes you told me I was being a 'typical boy' and sort of praised me for it and other times you beat me within an inch of my life."

George pursed his lips. "I had to do what I had to do. I thought if I kept you off-guard, you might quit."

"Right. By then trying to control everything else in my life. School, friends, girlfriends, activities, sports. You never passed up the opportunity to point out how much of a failure I was because I wasn't as good a jock as you had been. And bragged about your athletic achievements all the time. Way to make everything about you."

George's Glory Days parenting, expressed among physical beatings, tacit approval of Mike's behavior, and clear message that being a star athlete was more important to George than Mike was as a person, as well as his rather public violations in his marriage, helped to create in Mike a highly controlling personality. As we worked together it became obvious Mike always had to be right and would argue infinitely with anyone who didn't immediately agree with him or phrase things exactly as he demanded. Both Mike and George were stubborn and often threatened one another with violence. Both had permits to carry concealed weapons, so I made a rule they couldn't bring guns into my office. Oddly, and to my profound relief, they complied.

They continue to battle. Every once in a while I hear from one or the other of them complaining about the behavior of the other. George has violated Mike's boundaries with women repeatedly but has been ultimately rejected by the women, which has made him more aggressive with each contact. Mike has been encouraging his mom to divorce George, but she refuses. Mike has been engaged twice since our last meeting and has broken both relationships with his lying, cheating, and controlling behavior.

Theirs is a complicated, intense, and competitive relationship unlikely to change because both of them get something out of the relationship just as it is. They are emblematic of one of the great truths about people:

**People only change when they get
so uncomfortable with where they are that
change seems less scary.**

Neither George nor Mike is uncomfortable enough to change, and unless and until they get so uncomfortable with where and how they are that the effort to make a change is less stressful, they won't. Each of them gets something—no matter how dysfunctional or maladaptive—out of their relationship.

Obviously this is an extreme case, but I used it because it's also a vivid example of a worst-case scenario of Glory Days parenting and the possible result of such an approach as the child became an adult.

Both George and Mike are narcissists. We'll delve into narcissism and other personality disorders in Chapter 12, but briefly, narcissists see themselves as above others around them. They believe rules don't apply to them and that they deserve special treatment. They lie. Above all, they lack empathy or compassion and are divorced from their emotions. They operate only from ideas, not feelings. When you don't incorporate emotions or compassion into your choices, you can talk yourself into any behavior or action being fine.

George has told himself it's okay for him to cheat on his wife because he's attractive or charming or an athlete or just deserves to do what he wants. He doesn't consider the impact of his behavior on his wife and certainly not on his children or on the women with whom he cheats because he doesn't have empathy and can't feel what others do. He is satisfied, so that's absolutely all that matters to him.

Mike thinks his resentment of George and the competition between them justifies his actions—prior or present. His narcissism allows him to justify his criminal and promiscuous behavior. What sounds like concern for his mother's and sister's feelings is actually his understanding of which of George's buttons to push. These two are locked in narcissistic combat and neither will ever win.

Glory Days parents also play a verbal game of "I can top your story." No matter what experience someone has had, the Glory Days parent has had a similar but better one that they are quick to tell. They can't bear to be out of the spotlight even for a moment. So they may embellish their story—or even make it up, whatever it takes to be one of the crowd.

Acceptance is their goal, and their target group for acceptance replicates the age at which they felt most "loved" and accepted: their glory days.

If you are the child of a Glory Days parent, you need strong boundaries and good communication skills. It's a real temptation to confront and call out a Glory Days parent in the moment in which he or she is exaggerating or dominating or intruding. Instead, respectful diplomacy one on one is likely to be more productive.

"Mom, it's really not okay with me for you to spend so much time with my friends. I feel mad when you try to take over my friends' and my time together. I need you to be my mom, not one of my crowd." (Three sentences, remember?)

She is likely to respond with either defensiveness or anger. Don't let her hijack the conversation. Instead, stay with your point and stay calm. What you don't want to do is to get into an argument. You want to be heard and, more important, to set a boundary. If necessary, repeat what you've already said. And you might have to do it several times. Then offer a compromise: "Mom, I'd like for us to have a relationship with just the two of us so that we could spend more time together as mother and daughter." You have to be willing to live up to your offer, so don't say that if you're not, but if you are, it may be the deal maker.

Breathe and don't engage!

One of the founding fathers of psychology, Alfred Adler, said (and I'm paraphrasing here), "When dealing with difficult people, be firm, fair, and friendly." Be firm—keep your boundaries tight and don't allow yourself to be manipulated. Be fair—don't ask for the moon and don't offer what you're not willing to do. Be friendly—not buddy-buddy but warm and respectful. People hear you better when they are treated with kindness.

If you recognize yourself as a Glory Days parent, it's important for you to break your need to relive the past instead of celebrating the present and enjoying your life. It's important to live in the now. It's important to be mindful of whom you are, where you are, and in what stage of life you are.

Being present and mindful means you will develop healthy peer friends with whom you can share not only your past but your current life.

Open lines of communication with your kids—and young adults—that allow a new relationship to evolve in which you can be parent and child, adult to adult. There are lines you cannot and should not cross, chief among them the boundary of trying to compete with your children. They need you to be the wise adult to whom they can go for guidance, not the aging jock or cheerleader who's trying to inject him- or herself into their friendships or be in competition.

Acceptance of whom and where you are in life is sometimes a challenge, particularly in this youth- and beauty-obsessed culture, but it is necessary and appropriate to be an adult in the adult world, particularly for the benefit of your children.

On the other hand, if you are the child of a Glory Days parent, your best tools are good boundaries and a willingness to communicate with them— clearly, respectfully, appropriately, repetitively . . . and in three-sentence chunks.

Explain there are consequences for bad choices and be clear about your willingness to enforce them. "Mom, I have plans with Michelle, Tanya, and Alyson tonight. I know you'd like to join us, but that's not going to be appropriate. They'll be meeting me here, and I know they'll be glad to say 'hi' before we leave." Mom may push back or pout or try to get the other girls to invite her to join, and you may have to be willing to embarrass her to reset the boundary. If you do, she will likely be mad and hurt. If you don't, she'll be joining you and your friends for this and many other evenings. It's not an easy position to be in but you will eventually be glad you acted.

10

Blame Gamers

It's your fault. It's always your fault. It's always been your fault, even when it couldn't possibly be your fault. The Blame Game parents need a scapegoat and you're it, even if you had absolutely nothing to do with whatever it is you're being blamed for. Sometimes the reasoning by which your fault is established is so convoluted you need a diagram and advanced math to figure it out, but it always ends up being your fault.

As we discussed in Chapter 3, Blamers look for someone to blame rather than a problem to solve. Blamers are looking for someone to be wrong so that they can feel good about themselves at the expense of someone else, and they really don't care if they leave hurt feelings in their wake. Gratification is the focus—theirs, not yours.

Blame Gamers not only want you to be wrong, they want people around the issue to choose a side and disloyalty is strongly discouraged. Their team recruiting process involves lots of manipulation, pitting one family member against another to choose sides and labeling them "Right" and "Wrong." The family message sounds like, "If you choose the wrong side, you'll pay," so the stakes are very high in this game.

It is not uncommon in Blame Gamer families for there to be a scapegoat. Generally that child will emerge fairly early, often for no discernible reason. The role is not based on birth order or gender or even behavior. It's not limited to large families or small families; even only children can have the role of scapegoat.

The job of the scapegoat is to validate the opinions of and accept the blame for everything that goes wrong in the family. "If Mary weren't so spoiled, we would have the money for the rest of the kids to go to camp." Mary is likely the least spoiled of the kids, but she is assigned the blame for the parents' lack of money to send their kids to camp. In this way, Mom and Dad not only have someone to be wrong so that they don't have to own any of their own mistakes, but they have recruited the siblings to be on their team against Mary.

Scapegoats may also be used by one parent against another, both in a marriage and if the parents are separated or divorced.

Eliza had two strikes against her in her family before she was even born. First, she was the product of an outside relationship between her mother and her mother's boss, a man with flaming red hair, a truth that wasn't revealed until the delivery room. Everyone else in her family was blonde. Eliza emerged with flaming red hair. She was also the youngest of five girls and very much unwanted by either of her parents.

Eliza's mother's husband allowed his name to be put on her birth certificate, so she became, in official eyes, his daughter. "He never let me forget I was the product of my mother's betrayal. Any time he was mad at my mother—which was most of the time—he would blame his anger on me and call me 'the little redhead bitch.' If my sisters happened to be taking his side in the argument, they would also call me 'the little redhead bitch.' Then he'd call my mom a 'whore.' It was awful."

Eliza went on, "There was more than one time when my dad would take me to my biological father's business and wait until customers came into the shop, then loudly announce he had brought 'the little redhead bastard child' to see what a loser her real father was. At least twice, he made my mom come along as well, humiliating me, my mom, and her former boss in front of a store full of customers. The poor guy finally sold his business and moved out of town. It was a really small town, and there was a lot of gossip.

"I was so relieved when my parents divorced. I thought the torment would be over, but not a chance. It actually got worse. My mom and my sisters blamed me because we didn't have any money. My mom blamed me for the divorce. My dad used me to carry his hateful messages to my mom. And then I would get punished for the messages."

Now in her late forties, Eliza has no relationship with either parent. One or another of her sisters will periodically call her. "It's so strange. They call to tell me Mom hates me or has taken me out of her will or Dad is asking why I don't come to visit him. The creators of blame and shame have shifted to my generation. It's like my sisters have enlisted as soldiers in my parents' armies so that they can carry on their one-sided war. They don't ask what I'm doing or about my husband or our son's health and well-being. They just deliver their abusive messages in the sticky sweet way Mom used to and then hang up."

Blame Gamer parents' objective is to feel powerful. They accomplish this by taking the power away from the scapegoat. This is different from abusive parents—whom we will talk about in Chapter 14—who often target all their children relatively equally. Blame Gamers choose one target, but here's the twist: The scapegoat is the obvious, visible target, but it turns out all the kids are involved. The nonscapegoat kids are required to, as Eliza put it, "enlist in my parents' armies." The consequences for disloyalty are made clear without a word being exchanged: You don't want to be the scapegoat, do you? They don't, so they enlist and the scapegoat remains the scapegoat.

If you are the family scapegoat, you already know it's a no-win situation. No matter how hard you try, you will not escape that role unless you take a firm stance. Set boundaries, say no, do not allow yourself to be abused or blamed.

Stay in the Solver spot. Ask the Magic Question: What do we need to do to solve this problem? Of course, the problem will always be identified as you, but don't relent. If they are unable to identify a problem requiring a collaborative solution, even after you have repeatedly tried to determine what the problem is, walk away. Refuse to play because it's just another way to make you the scapegoat and the problem all over again.

The very worst thing you can do is to try to defend yourself against the blaming, shaming attacks. Remember, you are not the problem, so you don't have anything against which to defend. Anything that sounds even vaguely like defense will intensify the blaming and shaming.

GASLIGHTING

Gaslighting is a toxic kind of manipulation of facts and information designed to make you question if you're losing your mind. The term is based on the 1944 film *Gaslight,* in which a husband, wanting out of his marriage, sets out to drive his wife crazy so that he can divorce her. It's a classic and well worth watching.

Gaslighting is a favorite tool of the Blame Gamer because it keeps you off balance. Let me give you an example.

You've gone out to lunch with Mom: your obligatory bimonthly guilt trip and opportunity for her to blame you for the troubles in her life. Oddly, however, she's upbeat and interested in what you have to say. Then, without warning or explanation, she gets up from the table and leaves. You go back to your office, stewing about what you might have said or done that set her off but can't think of anything. Just before you are ready to leave the office, your cell rings with the "mom" tone. You debate with yourself for a minute about whether to answer, then cave.

"So what was that about?" she says, anger erasing the preliminaries.

"What was what about?" you respond, confused.

"You just got up and left. You didn't say good-bye. You didn't say anything. I guess you paid the bill. I suppose you expect me to be grateful. I had to find my car."

You stare at the phone. "Mom, you left," but there's a part of you reviewing what you recall to make sure you didn't get it twisted around.

"I certainly did not. As usual, you won't admit your misbehavior."

You have been gaslighted. Mom has manipulated the facts and made you question your memory.

Gaslighting is not a one-event technique. Instead it's cumulative over a long period of time. Every time you question your memory or wonder if you've gotten confused, the manipulation is working on you.

Ultimately, gaslighting is about power and control. The gaslighter/ Blame Gamer wants you off balance because when you are, you're easier to manipulate—and when you are easier to manipulate, you're less likely to resist being blamed for things you have not done.

You do not deserve to be blamed or gaslighted. You are not losing your mind.

14 Signs You Are Being Gaslighted

1. You are constantly second-guessing yourself.
2. You ask yourself, "Am I too sensitive?" a dozen times a day.
3. You often feel confused and even crazy at work.
4. You're always apologizing to your mother, father, boyfriend, boss.
5. You can't understand why, with so many apparently good things in your life, you aren't happier.
6. You frequently make excuses for your parents' behavior to friends and family.
7. You find yourself withholding information from friends and family so that you don't have to explain or make excuses.
8. You know something is terribly wrong, but you can never quite express what it is, even to yourself.
9. You start trying to do things to avoid the put-downs and reality twists.
10. You have trouble making simple decisions.
11. You have the sense that you used to be a very different person—more confident, more fun-loving, more relaxed.
12. You feel hopeless and joyless.
13. You feel as though you can't do anything right.
14. You wonder if you are a "good enough" son or daughter.

—Robin Stern, PhD, *The Gaslight Effect*
Used with permission.

You are not to blame for other people's choices, and you are not responsible for what's wrong in their worlds.

So, if you are being gaslighted, what to do?

1. *Do not let it slide.* Confront the distortion—respectfully but directly. "Mom, that's not how I remember it. You got up and left, and I was surprised and hurt."

2. *Do not question your sanity or your memory.* Pay attention to all of your experiences, not just the ones with the gaslighter. It will be easy to see the relationship between the times you feel crazy and who's present.

3. Do not excuse or explain or try to hide the gaslighter's behavior. Their behavior is theirs to own and you are not responsible.

4. *Use positive self-talk to contradict the negative messages of the Blame Gamer/gaslighter.* "I am a joyful, hopeful person." "I deserve to be happy." "I am successful and lovable." Make up your own messages and write them on Post-it notes, then put them where you see them every day and read them out loud so that you hear the affirmations in your own head in your own voice.

5. *Limit your exposure to the Blame Gamer/gaslighter*—and let the person know you are limiting your time because of the distortions. Being direct may be hard, but it shines a light on their behavior and evens out the playing field, getting your power back.

6. *Continue to invite them to join you in the Solver spot.* It will be easy to identify real problems versus manipulations. Confront the manipulations and work to solve the real problems.

7. *Use good, clear communication techniques.* State how you feel about the circumstances. Stick with three sentences. Be respectful but do not allow yourself to be gaslighted or blamed. Remind yourself you are *not* the problem.

Blame Gamers want you to be the problem, to be wrong, to feel badly about yourself so that they can feel better about themselves. That is not how relationships work. Period.

11

Users and Other Emotional Vampires

You are not an ATM, a free taxi, an unpaid maid, a no-charge car rental agency, a hotel, or a free store. I'm not talking about the usual family back-and-forth of loaning money or clothes or the car or any other of the myriad things we exchange because we're family and it's there. Instead, in this chapter we're looking at families where taking is far out of balance and weighed down with expectations and obligations. And guilt. Lots and lots of guilt.

Erika was still in high school when she first began working with me. She explained she had to schedule carefully because she was working two part-time jobs as well as going to school and was looking for a third job. I asked if she was saving for something special.

"No, I have to pay my parents. You know, rent for the house, rent for the car, insurance. And I pay everyone's cell phone bills. And for food, of course."

I looked at her intake sheet, wondering if I had misread her age. Sixteen. Junior in high school.

"How long have you been doing this?"

"I got my first job when I was fourteen," she said, "so since then."

Erika is the middle child of five with two older brothers and two younger half-sisters. She went on to explain both parents worked full-time jobs, but

"They really like to go to the casino and to Las Vegas. My stepdad told me they supported me for my first thirteen years, so now it's my turn."

I asked if her brothers had the same obligations. "Well, Jeremy moved out as soon as he turned eighteen. He lives in his own apartment in St. Paul. He told my stepdad he wouldn't put in a dime after he moved out and he hasn't. He can't come to the house, and my mom has to sneak to see him. Paul still lives at home, but he keeps getting fired from jobs. He dropped out of high school when he turned sixteen. He sleeps a lot. And my sisters are eight and six, so they don't work." She laughed an uncomfortable laugh.

I asked how much of her earnings she kept for herself.

She shook her head. "None. That's not how it works. I owe them. They took care of me for thirteen years. I've only been paying back for two."

In essence, Erika was financially supporting her parents' gambling habits. She was taking home almost $500 per week from her jobs, and her parents were taking it all. Worse, Erika's mom was putting pressure on her to switch from attending high school to online school so that she "could work during the day and do the school stuff at night." She was able to resist but reported the pressure from her mom was immense.

Erika's parents are users. They treated their adolescent daughter as a source of additional income and support for the family . . . and for their trips to the local casino. I met with the parents for a session, and it did not go well.

"Help me understand Erika's role in the family," I said, trying to open the conversation with neutral respect.

"She does what kids are supposed to do: contribute to the household." Her stepfather, Don's, tone was matter-of-fact as though his statement made perfect sense.

"It seems to me she contributes quite a lot. About $2,000 a month."

He nodded. "That seems about right. It could be better." He caught my concerned look. "She mooched off us for thirteen years. She owes us."

"Do your other adolescent children work?" I tried to keep the edge out of my voice.

"Jeremy's gone," he waved his hand, dismissing the eldest. "And Paul . . . well, Paul has some problems keeping a job. He isn't very bright."

I shook my head. "So it all falls on Erika's shoulders. Does that seem fair?"

Don glared at me, but Erika's mom, Marie, answered. "Life isn't fair. We're a family. Family takes care of its own."

"Frankly, I think you're taking advantage of Erika. She's still a kid, and you're stealing her teen years."

They left long before the session ended. I was not surprised. Erika continued to come to therapy, and about four months later, packed up and moved to live with an aunt in Georgia, where she enrolled in high school and junior college simultaneously. When she graduated from high school, she emailed me to tell me she had joined the military and was going to go to college to finish a degree in computer science.

User parents see their kids as a resource far beyond normal contribute-to-the-family chores. Erika is unusual because the user behavior of her parents began when she was in her early teens and because she was the only child for whom the expectations of her parents were enforced. She's also unusual because she escaped.

The user has a sense of entitlement: He, she, or they believe they are owed money or time or objects by those around them. When confronted they become defensive and angry, responding that they are somehow owed what they demand, just as Erika's family had.

This sense of entitlement often arises in childhood from two possible sources. Either a child is completely indulged and develops the idea he or she is owed whatever comes to mind or eye, or the child is denied everything but the most basic needs and determines to make sure that experience in adulthood is not repeated. In both cases, the result is a sense of being owed.

Sometimes this entitlement is conferred on a spouse as well as a child or children as the user marries for money and financial security without making his or her own financial contribution to the marriage. If this is by agreement between the two, it's fine. If, however, the initial expectation by the nonuser is of a partnership, it becomes a user relationship. The whole arrangement can become more complex if the parents of the noncontributing partner decide they, too, should be beneficiaries of the arrangement.

Users can also be emotional vampires. In this situation the entitlement takes the form of emotional using. The child or children of these parents are burdened with the expectation they will provide unlimited emotional support and energy to the parents while getting none for themselves.

Phyllis has a room in her house for her beauty pageant trophies and crowns. The walls are covered with sashes documenting her titles. Adjacent to the trophy room is a huge closet holding her competition gowns and shoes. She still competes occasionally but her focus is now pageant coaching, and because of her success, she has many young, pretty clients who aspire to follow in her footsteps. She also has a husband and two kids: Her son, Mitchell, is fourteen, a bookish, overweight kid with acne, and her daughter, Kendall, is nine and has been competing in pageants since she was a baby. Her trophies are stored in plastic containers in the garage. Phyllis's husband, Rocco, was a professional athlete and owns a number of fast-food franchises.

I met the family because Phyllis and Rocco were separated. Rocco was very concerned about Mitchell's plummeting grades and Kendall's sassy disrespect of her grandparents and teachers.

Phyllis had brought Kendall to the session when Kendall explained her behavior. "I'm pretty, and pretty people don't have to be nice."

Phyllis looked horrified. "Where did you get that idea?" she asked, before I could.

"That's what Dad said. He said that's how Mom goes through life. She's pretty so she doesn't have to be nice."

I jumped in before Phyllis could say anything. "Do you think that's right?"

"Well, he's my dad. He knows."

I asked what else Dad had told her about Mom, and she blithely related a number of very unflattering and inappropriate statements Rocco had made both directly to her and in her presence about Phyllis. We spent several sessions reversing Kendall's thinking.

Meanwhile, I met with Rocco and confronted him.

"Okay, so I probably said some stuff around the kids, but they need to know who their mother really is. I don't have anyone I can talk to except the kids, so when they're with me, we talk about their mom. I mean, who else knows her as well as the kids?"

Rocco was being an emotional vampire to his children, using them to dump his pain and anger about the separation without thinking about the consequences of his choices.

Kids are often indirect in their response to emotional issues. They tend to act out "sideways" rather than being directly confrontational or angry. Kendall chose being sassy to adults while Mitchell showed his discomfort via his grades.

It's not only young kids who can be affected by emotional vampires. Adult children may find themselves under pressure to fill the emotional lives of their aging parents, particularly if a parent is widowed. It's natural for a widowed parent to turn to one's children for support initially, but widowed parents also continue to gain emotional support from friends and extended family as well. If a widowed parent focuses his emotional needs only on his children, or one of his children, boundaries need to be established.

Boundaries are critical with users and emotional vampires because they don't have any. Further, they really don't want to hear you say no or set boundaries for them. They want you to give them what they want or be able to dump on you without consequences or pushback. They feel entitled to use you in whatever way they want because you are their child and "you owe them."

You don't. It is not your responsibility to be an ATM or a taxi or used in any way. It's not your obligation to be the emotional dumping ground for a parent. It's your right to say no and mean it.

That's not always easy, particularly with a parent who is alone or lonely or for whom you feel sad. That's where the guilt comes in. "But I'm Mom's only social support" tears at your heart and self-creates an obligation. I'm not suggesting you just suddenly blow Mom off or cut Dad loose completely. That would be awful for all concerned. Instead, be clear with your boundaries and enforce them with respect. Encourage Mom to reach out to friends or Dad to resume his connections while still being there—with boundaries.

Clear communication is also critical. Remember, users and emotional vampires have been trained since early childhood that they either deserve everything or deserve nothing. Balance isn't part of their repertoire. Therefore, you need to communicate your feelings and intentions clearly in hope that they will hear you and understand your point.

Users and emotional vampires equate money and things with love. If they can't use it or spend it, it's not love. They have discarded feelings in favor of material considerations. Connecting them with you and your feelings requires patience, boundaries, and communication. If they do not respond over time, perhaps you should consider Erika's solution: distance and going your own way.

❧12❧

Mentally Ill and Personality-Disordered Parents

Mental illness affects not only those people who suffer directly from it but also the families who love them. Mental illness ranges from mild disruptions of routine due to life events to long-term, serious, and pervasive life-altering diagnoses. Everyone deals with mild disruptions of one kind or another, and while they may be intense at the time they are happening, they resolve eventually and life goes back to its usual rhythms. With serious, long-term mental illness, however, life for the sufferer and the family is changed forever.

First, a bit about psychological diagnosis in general. We use a five-part—called five-axis—diagnostic system. Axis I diagnoses can be thought of as disorders that can be treated with medication and have some biological basis: depression, anxiety, adjustment disorders (those life disruptions I mentioned), bipolar disorder, and schizophrenia all fall under Axis I, among others. Axis II diagnoses are called *personality disorders*. A personality disorder occurs when *who* you are creates significant problems in your life. I'm not talking about personality traits—Sandy is kinda pushy or Mark tends to be pretty negative or Pat is shy and a bit of an introvert—but about deep core personality styles that influence every aspect of a person's life and relationships in a negative way.

Personality disorders are exaggerated traits. The most common—and most difficult—personality disorders are encompassed in Axis II, Cluster B: Antisocial Personality Disorder, Borderline Personality Disorder, Narcissistic Personality Disorder, and Histrionic Personality Disorder. Personality disorders are primarily a product of life experiences with some influence of genetics, according to some recent studies, and generally are not responsive to medication.

Axes III, IV, and V address social, financial, experiential, and coping factors affecting the person. While they are important to the whole diagnostic picture, they aren't our focus here.

We look here at both Axis I and Axis II diagnoses and their impact on the lives of those who suffer with them as well as those who are around them.

AXIS I

Everybody goes through times of difficulty, frustration, sadness, or anxiety—or some combination of those feelings—at one time or another in their lives in response to events. If those feelings persist over a longer period of time than what we'd expect—weeks or months—therapy and maybe medications will help to move past the event and back to "regular life." We call these event-driven disruptions *adjustment disorders*. They tend to be shorter term—less than six months—and we think of them as reactive, as in a reaction to something unusual.

If you or a loved one is going through an adjustment disorder, what you or they most need is support. That may take the form of time spent together, talking, special outings, or making meals. Since adjustment disorders are reactive in nature, you know eventually things will return to "normal" and your relationship will be what it was, good or bad.

Longer-lasting or lifelong diagnoses tend to be more complicated. Depression, anxiety, bipolar disorder, or schizophrenia in a parent have probably been there since before you were born. You have grown up with a parent whose perspective on life is deeply influenced by his or her diagnosis and has been for a long time. These diagnoses tend to be cyclical in nature as they ebb and flow.

At our first meeting Katie was really angry with her mother, Marsha. "I had been trying to call her for more than a day. With her history of depression and suicide threats, I call her every day just to check in, but she wasn't answering so I went over to her house. She was in her bathrobe and pajamas sitting in the dry bathtub, playing with a knife. She wouldn't answer me when I asked if she was depressed and if she'd taken her meds. This just pisses me off. I understand she has depression and I get that it comes and goes, but this dramatic crap makes it really hard to be helpful."

I asked if Marsha had taken her meds and was safe.

"She's in the hospital and back on her meds. It's part of her pattern. She feels better and hates the side effects of the meds so she goes off them and then plummets. She'll threaten suicide or tell me in some indirect way she's suicidal. I usually call her therapist or psychiatrist but this time she fired her therapist and her psychiatrist is out of town, so I told her she could either get dressed and come with me or I was going to call 911 and she could go by ambulance. And she had to give me the knife. I took her to the ER. I know it sounds selfish, but I'm sick of it."

I told her she sounded frustrated, and we talked about the source of that frustration. She had been her mother's emergency caretaker from childhood.

"For a long time I thought her depression was my fault. She sort of said it was because she said she never got over her postpartum depression, after she had me. All these years I've had to weave my life around my mother's depression and I realize she's not only let me, she's demanded it. I have had opportunities for jobs in other cities, and she's guilted me into staying here. I was engaged but she drove him away with her needs and her crazy stuff just like she did my dad. And when it's not depression, it's anxiety attacks. She calls me in the middle of the night because she's having an anxiety attack. She won't take her meds or takes them when she's already in the middle of an anxiety attack and then it becomes my problem. I'm sick of it."

I think a lot of children of people with major depression, bipolar disorder, anxiety, or schizophrenia can relate to Katie's frustration. At what point could she say, "No, Mom, you need to work through this on your own," particularly with the threats and hints of suicide?

Neither Katie nor anyone dealing with a suicidal, depressed parent should have to be the crisis manager. Katie's willingness to step in has given Marsha not only permission but has created an obligation in Marsha's mind. Katie's daily phone calls, in-person welfare checks, and crisis interventions have allowed Marsha to quit taking her medications, fire her therapist(s), and be certain she would be "rescued" by Katie. Marsha stopped having to be responsible for her own depression and anxiety.

People who have manageable mental illness are ultimately responsible for taking care of themselves, which means taking their meds as prescribed and consistently, maintaining a relationship with a therapist and a psychiatrist, making and keeping their appointments, being aware of their mental health status, and accessing intervention or emergency services when necessary. Marsha is more than able to do all these things, but she has decided to put the burdens on Katie.

If you find yourself in Katie's situation with a parent with manageable mental illness who has abdicated his or her responsibilities, you can return the focus to the patient and go back to being an appropriate support system. Appropriate support is asking how the parent is doing, listening to the answer, and encouraging the parent to access the professionals with whom they work. Even if you are a trained mental health professional, you cannot be your parents' therapist. If you're not a trained professional, make sure your affected parent or parents work with the professionals with whom they have a relationship.

The same is true for parents with serious mental illness, such as a difficult-to-treat type of bipolar disorder or schizophrenia. With these more severe forms of mental illness, medication can be less effective and routines harder to enforce. The same boundaries apply, however. The parent must have a relationship with a therapist or program and a psychiatrist. They may even have to live in a managed setting such as an inpatient program or group home. For many children, I know this information is hard to read or to contemplate, but you know how bad things can get with your mentally ill parent and you know the emotional price you pay when they are having trouble. Let the professionals do their jobs.

A poor solution would be for you to try to be their case or care manager. Certainly in major cities and often in rural areas, there are public and private professionals and programs to help people with serious and persistent mental illness. One thing you can do is research in your area or your parents' area to locate these professionals and programs. Then turn the situation over to them as much as possible. Also engage the program professionals to take on the role of care/case manager rather than you if your afflicted parent isn't capable of making his or her own plans. You are most effective as the loving child who visits and brings treats, not as the care manager.

It's really tempting to think you can be your parent's care team, particularly if you have control issues. It's a temptation best resisted because it will exhaust you and, like Katie, can take over your life. I know it sounds cold, but your job is to be a son or daughter, not a treatment center. Crossing that line is not good for anyone involved.

AXIS II

The National Institutes of Health estimates about 15 percent of the general US population has some sort of personality disorder. Other studies have indicated as high a prevalence of personality disorders at 20 percent. These numbers don't matter if you are the child of a personality-disordered parent and experience the impact on your life. In your case, it's 100 percent and you have to deal with the effects.

As I noted above, the most prevalent and difficult personality disorders are those in Cluster B—Antisocial, Borderline, Narcissistic, and Histrionic—and we'll look at those in detail. Cluster A Personality Disorders are those that mimic schizophrenia or include people whose eccentricities set them significantly apart from others. Cluster C disorders are those of the anxious and fearful: Avoidant, Dependent, and Obsessive-Compulsive. Both Clusters A and C represent a very small portion of personality disorders.

Cluster B disorders, on the other hand, are much more prevalent—think one in about every six people—and create much more chaos in the lives of people around them.

Antisocial Personality Disorder

Antisocial Personality Disorder (APD) is characterized by criminal behavior, manipulation, lies, and, often, violence of one kind or another. About 3 percent of men and 1 percent of women in the overall population fit into this category, but about 85 to 90 percent of prison populations have APD. People with Antisocial Personality Disorder are emotionally cold and distant, although they are more than able to present a different face. Their ability to switch masks at will is part of what makes them dangerous. They are very good at reading people and present the façade that will get them what they want.

While certainly the classic image of the criminal—sneaky, violent, angry, scary lawbreakers—applies, Antisocial Personality Disorder also includes people who manipulate with charming, facile, and witty behavior, flattering their targets and playing with emotions, often arrogant, but totally lacking in real empathy or connections.

**Empathy is the ability to understand
another person's situation by being able
to put yourself in their shoes.**

These types of APD people rely more on subtle manipulation and control, although they can be violent and certainly do disregard the law without a sense of guilt or remorse. This subset is called *sociopathic*, and the more extreme versions are *psychopaths*. The cardinal trait of sociopaths and psychopaths is a complete and total lack of empathy. They see their targets as pawns in their games. Other people are only valuable if they can be used, and then discarded when their usefulness has expired.

Whether a classic criminal or a sociopath/psychopath, people with APD are dangerous to those around them—family or strangers. They tend to solve problems with violence—physical or emotional or psychological—and are always thinking of ways in which they can "win," which implies there will be someone who loses—their victims. People can be both classic narcissist and sociopathic APD at the same time, which makes them doubly dangerous.

A reminder: All criminals, including sociopaths, are not in prison. Indeed, some of the more successful sociopaths and psychopaths are in executive offices of corporations or government.

We want to believe and trust people who are charming. Everybody likes to feel liked, and charming people make us feel liked. And there are many people who are charming and who are *not* APD. Unfortunately, it's not often easy to tell at first meeting, which is what sociopaths/psychopaths count on. The essential difference between genuinely charming people and sociopaths comes down to intent. Truly charming non-APD people are consistent in their behavior over time and their intention is to make an emotional connection. The intention of sociopaths/psychopaths, on the other hand, is to manipulate their target using charm to get what they want without regard to what anyone else needs or wants.

Lies are a central feature of the APD personality. The lies are plentiful and designed to suck you in. They will use any information they've gleaned about you from observation or conversation. Some even do research before meeting you. They build their "story" around that knowledge so that you will believe them and cooperate with their goals. You absolutely cannot and should not trust them or believe them. Consequently, we need to lose some of our innocence in order to protect ourselves from charming con men and women—in short, to be more cynical.

If you are the child of someone who has Antisocial Personality Disorder, you have experienced the lies, manipulation, anger, violence—physical, sexual, psychological, verbal, emotional, financial—and the fake charm. You are probably very cynical and have major trust issues with everyone, even those who are not APD.

It is *impossible* to build trust with a person with Antisocial Personality Disorder. Lies are such an integral part of their behavior, and truthfulness and honesty are two of the building blocks of trust. The APD parent will attempt to recruit you to their "side" and possibly into their nefarious endeavors. You could be vulnerable to these efforts because they have been "working on" you from your earliest years, normalizing their behaviors and choices, making them seem rational and appropriate.

If the APD parent is incarcerated or in frequent legal trouble, it's a bit more clear their behaviors are to be avoided than it is with a sociopathic or psychopathic parent who operates from the boardroom or executive office. Unfortunately, because they operate in roles that appear to be "legitimate," their behaviors seem normal, even admirable. This is where you need to pay closer attention to their motivations and the outcomes of their behaviors.

We learn our morals and social rules at home first, but we also learn in the community. If you find yourself uncomfortable with the behaviors or choices of a parent who fits the qualities of the APD, particularly sociopaths or psychopaths, compare their behavior to that of people who you know and that you respect. Then use those people as role models rather than look to the APD person.

Having good boundaries is also essential because APD people are very determined to achieve their goals, and they don't care if that interferes with your life or goals. You will be under pressure, so keep your boundaries tight.

Also, don't defend their behavior. You have been carefully molded through your childhood and youth to be "loyal" and, consequently, to defend the behaviors of the APD parent to the rest of the world. If their behavior is at odds with that of the rest of society or if they are taking advantage of others or lack empathy or are uncaringly in defiance of the law, they are choosing their path and it is not your job to defend behaviors with which you do not agree or actually oppose. Defending the indefensible is not loyalty. It's complicity, and it makes you part of the problem.

Remember, you have the right and the power to say no. APD parents, and APD persons in general, do not want to hear "no" in most cases. It goes back to the loyalty they want. They expect you to follow their plan without question, so saying no and meaning it may very well draw their wrath. Hence, you need to be prepared to stand your ground or walk away.

Ultimately, it's very important to remember it is *impossible* to have a genuine relationship with a person with Antisocial Personality Disorder.

You do not have the magic to change them, fix them, convert them, teach them, or love them out of it. They are deeply damaged beings and are in their version of survival mode. The results of attempting a relationship with them will only damage you.

Walk away and stay away.

Borderline Personality Disorder

Borderline Personality Disorder (BPD) is primarily characterized by an exaggerated fear of abandonment. I'm not talking about the kind of fear most of us would have of being abandoned because we might not be safe but rather fear of being abandoned because they will not know who they are.

People with Borderline Personality Disorder make up about 6 percent of the overall population. Male and female borderlines exist, but the diagnosis tends to be skewed in the direction of women, just as APD tends to be skewed toward men. It may seem like a diagnostic bias, but by observation over my nearly thirty-year career I have seen this reflects reality.

Borderlines often have abusive childhoods that have required them to adopt behavioral extremes to manage their feelings. Their relationships are unstable, as are their jobs and finances. They tend to create drama and chaos in their own lives and the lives of those around them. Drug and alcohol abuse are common problems. Borderlines have a sense of desperation around them that sometimes leads them to self-harm with cutting or overdoses or suicide attempts. Suicide threats are also a common manipulative technique used to get their way. A significant percentage of persons with BPD have a history of childhood sexual abuse. This is not to say all persons who suffered sexual abuse in childhood have BPD, but rather childhood sexual abuse is often a contributing factor in the development of BPD.

Life with a BPD parent is unpredictable. One moment they may be lavishing love and attention on you, and the next you are the worst person who ever lived—and you have done nothing in the interim. Parents with BPD go to extremes often because they have a great deal of trouble managing their emotions. They may not be aware of their emotions, so they exaggerate them to become visible emotionally to themselves and others.

If you are the child of a parent with BPD, you first need to learn your own feelings and be able to manage them without extremes. As we talked about in Chapter 2, you begin with the basics: mad, glad, sad, and scared. It's important to be aware of how you feel in any given situation as well as to be able to understand and interpret how others feel based on their words, actions, and body language. Persons with BPD do not have these skills, so you will have to do this work on your own or with a therapist.

As with everything, you will need strong boundaries to manage your relationship with a borderline parent. In addition to saying "no" and meaning it, one effective technique is for you to set your goals for any interaction and stick to those goals. The BPD parent will want to wander to other topics or distract with emotional outbursts, so your job is to firmly bring the subject to your set goal and pursue it. Don't let yourself get distracted or carried along on a tsunami of exaggerated emotions. Come back to your goal.

Be a Solver. Borderlines are not looking for a solution. Instead they are looking for what is comfortable and familiar to them: chaos. As we have previously discussed, chaos and solutions are mutually exclusive. In order for you to achieve your goal, you need to firmly plant your emotional feet in the Solver spot and stay there with determination.

Use clear emotional language with a BPD parent. Because they are listening for any hints of abandonment, they may not pay attention to whatever else you have to say. Keeping it simple means your communication is more likely to be heard and less likely to trigger an exaggerated response. If you get an exaggerated emotional response, stop and come back to your conversation when things have calmed down. You will never accomplish any resolution or even problem identification in a chaotic situation.

Unfortunately, being raised by someone with BPD means you may have a quick trigger with that parent. If she explodes, it may trigger you to explode. Therefore, it's extremely important for you to feel in control of your own emotions and stay in control in interactions with your BPD parent. Remember, if the situation gets out of control, nothing will be accomplished and the borderline will feel right at home.

Here's the good news. There is a very effective treatment protocol for BPD called dialectical behavioral therapy (DBT). The therapy is conducted in group, often with additional therapy one on one. DBT is a series of exercises in blocks designed to teach participants emotional management skills. Generally the entire course runs about a year, with group sessions once or twice a week. DBT is very effective with adolescents and adults, and I have recently learned that DBT is being used with children who have issues with emotional and behavioral self-control. Most mental health clinics have a therapist who is trained in DBT, and it is covered by many insurance plans. DBT, like all effective tools, takes time, practice, and commitment. If you can encourage your BPD parent to participate, it can really improve your chances for a healthy relationship.

DBT is also a great skill set for children of borderlines to learn how to effectively deal with a BPD parent. If your borderline parent won't go, you might consider it for yourself.

Some excellent books are available to help you manage BPD people, and they appear in the bibliography at the end of this book.

Narcissistic Personality Disorder

Narcissistic Personality Disorder is characterized by an exaggerated sense of one's own importance, grandiosity, a lack of compassion or empathy, manipulation, exaggeration, lack of remorse, no real emotions—only intellectual mimicry of emotions—pathological lying, unwillingness to accept responsibility for their own behavior, and a belief they are superior to everyone else. About 6 percent of the overall population—one person in fifteen—has diagnosable Narcissistic Personality Disorder, according to statistics from a number of studies. Sometimes the percentage seems much higher.

Most everyone is a little bit narcissistic, and it's a necessary survival tool. Perhaps the most narcissistic people in the world are babies. They have no compassion for their overtired parents and believe themselves to be the center of the universe. It's how babies survive: They make it impossible to ignore their needs, and they don't care about the consequences to others. Fortunately, the majority of people learn compassion and, by their mid-teens, move beyond narcissism.

As you read the characteristics, narcissists sound a lot like Antisocial Personality Disordered persons, particularly sociopaths and psychopaths, and sometimes it's hard to tell the difference because they are similar, particularly in the extreme versions of both diagnoses. One difference is the amount and degree of criminal behavior exhibited by persons with Antisocial Personality Disorder, but it can be a fine line. Perhaps the most clarifying difference is intent. APD people manipulate others for personal gains monetarily or materially while narcissists manipulate others to feel better about themselves.

Narcissists tend to behave like middle schoolers: bullying, gossiping, intense self-focus, lack of empathy or compassion, manipulating, lying, and difficulty accepting responsibility are all early adolescent behaviors. You can think of a narcissist as being stuck at about age twelve or thirteen.

Narcissists are also divorced from their feelings. Rather than experiencing and exhibiting genuine feelings, they intellectually mimic emotions without actual feelings attached. If you stay only in your intellect without accessing your emotions, you can get into some very dark behaviors. Without compassion and feelings to moderate behavior, people are capable of terrible things. Child abuse, sexual abuse of children or adults, emotional abuse, and psychological abuse are all part of the narcissist's capability. Again, the narcissist and someone with Antisocial Personality Disorder seem to fall into the same bucket. The difference comes down to intent and motive.

Narcissists are in competition with everyone around them, and they desperately need to "win." Winning, to a narcissist, means complete domination of their target. In order for them to win, you have to lose and they need to believe they are the agent of that loss. They need to feel superior to everyone, and winning represents that superiority. Combine that with a lack of remorse or compassion, and you can imagine the potential for damage, particularly to a child.

One common tool for a narcissist is the put-down. Because they stay in their intellect, they spend a lot of time and energy accumulating information about you they can later turn into a zinger against you, almost always at the worst possible time.

"It's too bad you gained all that weight back after your surgery. Of course, you weren't strong enough to lose it without help in the first place. That's what happens to weak people." And then the "smirk" as your eyes tear up and you feel terrible. The narcissist has won because you have lost and he or she can see your tears, making them feel victorious.

Another favorite technique is gaslighting. We talked about it in Chapter 10, but to refresh your memory, in gaslighting the narcissist flips reality, turning a situation upside down.

For example, you have asked your narcissistic mom to help you with your kids while you are helping with your cousin's wedding, and she has agreed enthusiastically.

"If you come and bring the kids, you have nothing to worry about. We'll take care of it all." So you show up, kids in tow, and search the wedding venue for your mom. She is nowhere to be found, and your little people are, as prekindergarteners tend to, running amok. When your narcissistic mom shows up right before the ceremony, you are frazzled and have not been able to help your cousin as you'd planned.

"Mom," you say with obvious irritation, "I thought you were going to take care of the kids so I could help Stacey."

"I never said any such thing. You know my back is giving me trouble. I would never agree to do that."

Later you overhear her in conversation with one of her friends, describing the wedding. "Well, I would have enjoyed it much more, but my daughter just dumped her kids on me and I had to step up and take care of them."

You feel crazy, and that's the whole point of gaslighting: If you feel crazy, the narcissist has won.

Verbal, sexual, financial, spiritual, emotional, physical, and psychological forms of abuse are other techniques narcissists use to put you in the loser position. What the narcissist wants is to undermine your confidence and your sense of self. They want you to question your life and experiences and find yourself wanting. They want you weak, insecure, self-doubting, confused, and needy. They want to be in control.

You might be familiar with passive-aggressive behavior. It used to be a standalone personality disorder diagnosis but has now been included in Narcissistic Personality Disorder. Passive-aggressive behavior is another form of manipulation.

"It certainly would be nice if my son called me once in a while [sigh]."

"It's really sad when someone you love takes advantage of you [sigh]."

Passive-aggressive manipulation puts you on the defensive immediately, even if you haven't done anything wrong. It also puts the narcissist firmly in the victim spot and you in the role of perpetrator.

Relationships with narcissists don't start out with abuse. Instead they seduce you to see them as wonderful, loving people. They lavish attention and caring on you until you are really hooked, and then they begin eroding your confidence, bit by bit, using some or all of the techniques described above.

If you are the child of a narcissist, your other parent has likely been "eroded" by the relationship and may have trouble standing up for you because they can't stand up for themselves. The narcissist will be in competition with you from early on, needing the spotlight and resentful when you, with your cute baby self, take it away.

You have at that moment begun the lifelong competition that will take many forms over the years, including taking credit for your achievements while implying or directly saying that the narcissist is responsible for your ability to achieve in the first place. The narcissist may be in competition with you for your friends or significant others. He or she certainly will be in competition with you for the attention of the other parent, particularly if your parents are divorced.

Narcissists don't coparent. They compete, control, abuse, bully, gaslight, use, and manipulate not only the other parent but also the children. And if they don't get what they want, they escalate until they do. They use their children as messengers, ploys, and tools to keep the other parent off balance. They exhibit no compassion or thought for the damage they are doing to their kids or the relationship with the kids.

Unlike "average" people, narcissists see relationships as tools to get what they want from the world without making any emotional contribution. Emotions are mimicked but not genuinely felt by them, but they're good actors and we want to believe them because they're charming, even though the charm is inauthentic.

Then, when you have hit your breaking point and have decided to just walk away, they hook you back in with loving words and kind gestures or acts that make you think you must be the problem because the narcissist is obviously wonderful. As soon as they feel you are securely back in their sphere, the put-downs and abuse begin again. The "trap" behaviors are theater designed to keep you interested and involved.

As with the other Cluster B personality disorders, dealing with a narcissist is difficult and exhausting. Of course, good, solid boundaries are mandatory, as is a thick skin and the ability to say "no" and mean it. Narcissists lay out a lot of bait to entice you into playing their games. *The only way to win with a narcissist is not to play.*

Instead, as with borderlines, you set the relationship goals and stay firmly in the Solver spot. Do not accept blame for things you have not done. Do not give the narcissist free rent in your head. Use positive affirmations— true statements that reflect the ideal you want to achieve—to repair your damaged sense of self. Work with a good therapist who understands narcissists so that you have a support system that doesn't allow the negatives to stick. A list of excellent books about dealing with narcissists appears in the bibliography of this book.

Be your own person. And if the narcissism is toxic, be prepared to walk away.

Histrionic Personality Disorder

Histrionic Personality Disorder is characterized by very exaggerated emotional responses to relatively mundane situations. The objective of the overreaction is to get attention. Some people refer to this as "Dramatic Personality Disorder." People with this personality disorder need to be the center of attention but not in the way narcissists do because histrionic people are overly in touch with their emotions and express them very visibly. People who are histrionic have an excessive need for approval from others. About 2 percent of people are histrionic—the majority, though not all, female.

You never have to wonder what a histrionic person is feeling. They will tell you, usually in exaggerated terms. They're not just happy, they're ecstatic! They're not just sad, they're devastated! Something is not just big, it's huge! Hyperbole is the norm. As a result, people tend to ignore their adjectives after a while. When they become aware they are no longer the center of attention, the hyperbole and quest for the spotlight increase.

If you are the child of a histrionic parent, you are used to the drama. Everything has been too big your whole life. You have reacted in one of two ways: You are either very quiet and introverted, or you have responded in kind and exaggerate your emotions in an effort to be emotionally visible to your histrionic parent and others.

If you have chosen the quiet, more introverted path, you are probably very uncomfortable around your histrionic parent or anyone with that behavior.

Melinda's mom, Lillian, is the frequent headliner in their local community theater—and larger than life in her speech, dress, actions, and conversations. Melinda, on the other hand, is a quiet, thoughtful woman who takes guitar and French lessons in anticipation of a trip to bicycle through the south of France. She is very uncomfortable with Lillian's theatrical and flamboyant ways but would like to have some relationship with her mom.

Unfortunately, Lillian considers Melinda's avoidance of her productions an insult and becomes angry with Melinda, zinging her whenever they are together, then pretending it was a "joke" and accusing Melinda of having no sense of humor.

Melinda and I worked together and devised a plan of action. Rather than shrinking away from Lillian's phone calls and visits, Melinda would create a structured activity—like going to a costume exhibit at a local museum—they would both enjoy.

If Lillian made any of her "jokes," Melinda would gently confront her: "Mom, you might have meant that as a joke but it really hurt my feelings." I encouraged Melinda to lower her expectations for Lillian's behavior toward her so that she would not be so upset when Lillian acted in her flamboyant and theatrical way. We also agreed she would keep in touch with Lillian between visits by texting her about once a week with all Melinda's news.

It didn't work perfectly, but our plan worked. Lillian actually suggested several things they could do together that were interesting to both of them. The zingers didn't stop entirely, but they slowed down and Melinda was able to confront them. The remaining sticking point is Melinda's reluctance to go to the theatrical productions, but she has agreed to go once and try to set aside her own discomfort. She even suggested she might take flowers for Lillian.

If you are the quiet child of a histrionic parent, you might adapt Melinda's plan for yourself. Boundaries, as always, are critical, as is assertive behavior.

> Assertiveness is the ability to set clear boundaries with another person while allowing both yourself and the other to keep their personal power. It's asking for what you want without taking away from someone else.
>
> Aggressiveness is getting what you want at the expense of someone else. It's demanding what you want no matter the cost to another.

Assertiveness is always the Solver's choice. It's fine to ask, directly, for what you want and need and then be willing to negotiate to a resolution everyone involved can agree to.

When you're dealing with a histrionic person, you have to be emotionally visible to them in order for them to make a connection. Don't fall into the trap of trying to outdrama them. Instead, stick to finding a solution to one problem at a time with a goal of finding a working compromise where you and your histrionic parent both get a bit of what you want.

You might remember that earlier I paraphrased Alfred Adler, one of the three founders of modern psychology. He said, essentially, "When you are dealing with difficult people, be firm, fair, and friendly." *Firm* means to have good boundaries and be in control of yourself. *Fair* means to keep the interests of both sides in mind. *Friendly* means to be open but not to allow yourself to be taken advantage of. Dr. Adler's advice is really good when you are dealing with a parent with a personality disorder.

﴾13﴿

Addicted to _____

Just as the children of mentally ill and personality-disordered parents have major challenges dealing with the effects of the parents' choices, so also do those people whose parents are addicted to substances or behaviors.

"Addiction" is a term that gets thrown around to cover a multitude of behaviors from shopping to gambling to hard drugs. In my mind, the word "addiction" describes substances that create a physical craving and lead to further use. Behaviors like excessive shopping and gambling are, to me, more coping mechanisms to manage anxiety or depression. In either case, however, the use of substances or behaviors takes over the life of the user and creates chaos for their families.

We are in the middle of a drug addiction epidemic worldwide. Not only drugs like heroin or cocaine but also synthetic, lab-created drugs like methamphetamines or ice or krokodil have been joined by overuse and abuse of prescription drugs like fentanyl or oxycontin. Alcohol continues to be a problem as well.

The whys of addiction are complex and have been covered in great depth in the helping literature. Genetics plays a role as does environment, but there are people who are genetically predisposed to addiction and whose environmental elements virtually encourage it, yet they resist. There are also those unfortunate people who may have a weak or nonexistent genetic predisposition for addiction who get hooked. It's not an exact science, which makes addiction all the more complicated. For whatever reason people end up addicted to substances or behaviors, the consequences to their children are often lifelong.

When you are dealing with someone who is addicted, you are never going to be their top priority. The substance or behavior tops everything else. Second priority is usually making sure they have a supply, and third is often the using relationships—the friends with whom they associate because of their common use. Fourth is recovery from the last use. All of those priorities mean the best you can place on the list of importance is fifth, which is not a desirable place to be in someone's life in which you want and need to be a top priority.

In addition, the behaviors of a person whose consciousness is altered due to substance abuse are often unpredictable at best. Violence, verbal abuse, sexual abuse, emotional abuse, name-calling, and abandonment all can be part of the addict's behavioral constellation. Any one or more of these is damaging with one incident, but when you are dealing with someone who is addicted, it's unlikely to be only one incident. Much more likely is that the negative behaviors will repeat again and again. The repetition of abuse compounds its effects on the victim, making it harder to recover.

Beth's road to adulthood was rocky at best. Her father, an executive, was a social drinker whose alcohol consumption increased as his corporate responsibilities and stresses increased.

"At first my dad was a mellow drunk, but when his job got tougher, he got mean. Then my mom had her car accident and got hooked on painkillers. She spent a lot of time in bed or stoned and staring out the window. The more she retreated, the angrier my dad got, and the angrier he got, the more he yelled at me. My sister and brother hid from Dad, but I couldn't do that. Instead, I yelled back. And I ran away, stole stuff, took drugs, hung out with bad friends, and got arrested. I must have seen twenty different therapists, and I didn't let any of them help me. Of course that made my dad even more mad and my mom even more stepped back. Finally a judge gave me a choice of going to treatment or going to juvie until I was eighteen. Since I was fourteen at the time, I figured I could game treatment just like I did the therapists, so I chose treatment. I was there for three years. I wish I could say it turned my life around completely, but that's a movie plot. I did get off drugs and have mostly stayed off since. I also learned a lot about managing my anger, but I'm far from perfect there either. What I didn't learn until much later was about relationships."

Beth was in her early thirties when she came to therapy following her second divorce. She has two preteen sons and a younger daughter. "Amy is, unfortunately, the same kid I was. She's defiant, angry, and confrontational. Mark and Jim are cautious around her since she has beaten each of them up at least once. The boys' dad is addicted to painkillers—so my first husband was just like my mom. Amy's dad is just like my dad: alcoholic, verbally abusive, angry, and resentful—so the second husband I married was just like my dad. I'm here to change my path for the next man in my life."

"What about just changing your path for yourself and your kids?"

Beth's eyebrows raised and she looked at me. "I told you I was good at the game."

"If you want to play games, I'm not the therapist for you."

She thought for a minute, clearly having an inner dialog, then nodded. "I guess I've tried games and they didn't work. Maybe it's time for me to get to work." And she did.

Beth's analysis of her first two marriages affirms an old saying: We first marry the parent with whom we have the most issues. Unfortunately, she had two damaged parents to choose from, so she chose one of each.

The retreat of her mother left Beth unprotected from her father's rages, so rather than hiding as her brother and sister did, she became aggressive and confrontational. "I did everything I could to make my dad mad, but one thing I learned in treatment was I was trying to make him pay attention to me. I got his attention, but it wasn't the kind of attention I needed. I felt completely alone in the world, and I still do in a lot of ways. I don't trust anyone, including myself. I don't want my kids to struggle like I did, but I don't think I give them what they need. I yell too much. My temper is short, and I call them names. Yes, I married my parents, but I did as much to screw up the marriages as my husbands did."

What Beth describes is not unusual for children of addicts or alcoholics. Beth's priority with her dad was sixth or seventh at best because of his job and his anger with her mom. She learned to distrust rather than trust. She works at her sobriety but admits sometimes she gets drunk "just to be able to let go. I have to try to be in control all the time, and it's exhausting."

There are no magic solutions for Beth. Like anyone seeking to overcome hurdles, she has to be determined and focused but also learn how to forgive herself for her mistakes.

The idea of forgiveness of self and others as a part of healing has been getting a second look lately, and the idea of blanket forgiveness of those who have damaged us is being replaced by the idea of forgiveness in response to an apology. The thought behind this perspective is that forgiveness without ownership by the perpetrator actually revictimizes the victim, again putting them in a one-down position.

Obviously, there are certainly situations in which an apology will never be forthcoming—if the abuser is deceased or absent or refuses to acknowledge his or her behavior. It seems to me that getting to the point where one feels free of the effects of another's behavior is the most effective path. If you can get acknowledgment and an apology, by all means do so. If not, do what you need to do to release yourself from the binding you did not create.

In Beth's case, her mom and dad divorced while Beth was in treatment, further estranging them for a time. Eventually, her mom went to treatment for her painkiller addiction, and the two have been able to build a relationship. It's far from perfect. Beth's mom lives in California and her contact is sporadic. When she comes to visit, she lavishes the kids with attention and gifts and incessantly gives Beth child-rearing advice.

Beth's dad, on the other hand, continues to abuse alcohol and steadfastly deny he was ever abusive. He lives locally, and Beth hasn't seen him or spoken to him for several years. She has no interest in reconnecting.

Beth's sister abuses a variety of drugs and has been in and out of jail and treatment. They are rarely in touch, usually only when her sister needs bail money or some other sort of rescue. Beth's brother has cut off the entire family, and she has no idea where he is or if he is even alive. Nobody in Beth's family has escaped the ravages of alcohol and drug abuse by the parents.

One of the most important lessons Beth has had to learn—and, if you are the child of an addict of one sort or another, you will need to learn—is not to get sucked into the Fixer role. Addicts will try to engage you for the purpose of getting their needs met, using guilt—a powerful weapon—to manipulate you into making your lives easier. They use all the Player techniques to put you into the Fixer position. You must remember that "no" is a complete sentence, and shame is a maladaptive tool designed to make you feel badly about yourself and your situation. They use shame to try to make you feel badly about yourself so that your self-esteem will drop and you will do what they want.

**Guilt is feeling badly because of
something you have done. Shame is feeling
badly because of who you are.**

Dealing with addicted parents will involve a lot of saying "no" and setting firm boundaries because their addiction is driving their behavior, and as long as they are addicted, the substance or behavior will be in charge.

Sometimes the substance or behavior will still be in charge even if the parent has stopped using. In alcohol treatment terms, it's called being a "dry drunk." What that means is the use may have stopped, but the parent has not changed anything else and is still angry or abusive or difficult. It's the illusion of sobriety without actual change, and it's a lie.

Change is difficult. People in general take the line of least resistance, which means they may talk about making changes or even claim to have made changes, but in truth, nothing has really happened because change is hard work and takes a long time. The mythology is it takes twenty-one days to make a new habit. The truth is much less optimistic. Studies indicate the more radical the change, the longer it takes to create the habit, and it's often months or years for things like addictions.

Let's take a minute to talk about behaviors that get included in the addiction bucket. Shopping, gambling, spending, eating, sex, gossip, or any other repetitive actions that dominate a person's focus can have similar negative effects on families. I prefer to think of them as ineffective attempts to self-medicate.

The economic impact of overspending or gambling is obvious, but the more subtle consequences of any self-medicating behaviors are also damaging to relationships because the actor is taking attention and energy from the relationships to give to the behavior, abandoning the needs of the family and the children to medicate their own issues with the repetitive behaviors.

Kids who feel abandoned or neglected will either try to become invisible, like Beth's siblings, or highly noticeable, as Beth did. What they don't or can't do is to parent themselves.

If you are the child of an addict, or worse yet, addicts, you have a hill to climb to escape the effects of their choices on your life. Perhaps the most important step is to stop either blaming yourself for their choices— although they may have blamed you—or trying to fix them and everyone else in your life.

You didn't break them, you can't fix them.

It's really easy for the child of an addict to jump into the Fixer role and try to make everything right, but when you are tempted to do that, remember:

1. "No" is a complete sentence.
2. They really don't want you to make anything work, they just want what they want with the least effort.
3. You are accustomed to being manipulated, so it will feel both familiar and right, although it is not.
4. Guilt is about something you may have done. If you haven't done anything, you are not guilty. Not being codependent is strength, not wrong action.

5. Shame, another favorite weapon, is about who you are. You are not the problem and do not deserve to be made to feel badly about yourself.

Instead of being the Fixer, be the Solver. Have boundaries and keep them strong. Ask them to join you in identifying a problem and finding an equitable solution. Most of all, don't get sucked into their drama.

There's an old Russian saying that bears repeating:
Not my circus, Not my monkeys.

If you find yourself drawn into dramas of addicts' creation, remind yourself of this wisdom. Repeatedly.

A really important element for your healing is support from healthy people. Growing up in an addicted, chaotic household won't give you a model for what healthy people and relationships look like and how they behave. Seek sober people as friends and observe their interactions to learn what they do differently from your family of origin, then try their approaches to the world. I'm not saying sober people have all the answers or are undamaged, but their damage will be different than yours and you can work together to heal your wounds and support each other.

Another place to find support, if you are comfortable with twelve-step models, is to attend Adult Children of Alcoholics (ACOA) meetings. At these meetings you will find people who have had experiences similar to yours and are in the process of figuring out how to get past their hurdles. There is great wisdom available in connecting with people who have walked on similar paths and are in different stages of their healing.

Additionally, you might want to explore therapy. Find a therapist who understands family dynamics and addictions. Don't quit therapy when you get uncomfortable. Discomfort is a great motivator for change because as long as you're comfortable, you're not likely to do the hard work change requires. In therapy you want to learn how to connect with your own emotions effectively, as well as how to read emotions in others. You will also learn trust, a very important element. And your self-esteem will grow as you learn new tools and feel more confident.

Finally, recognize it's a process. You're not going to be perfect. You're not going to get it right every time. The addicts will do what they will do, and you won't be in control. But as long as you're working on you and taking care of yourself and growing, you're doing the best you can for yourself, and celebrate that.

14

Abusive Parents

Abuse takes a lot of different forms, all of them damaging to children. In the last chapter we talked about abuse as connected to addictions of one sort or another, but there is, sadly, abuse that occurs without addictions as well.

Abuse can be physical, sexual, spiritual, psychological, verbal, emotional, or a combination of any or all of them. The intent of abuse, regardless of form, is taking the power and control away from the victim.

Physical abuse can take the form of everything from slapping or pinching or hair pulling to beatings and confinement in scary or dirty places.

Sexual abuse is not only a physical act of sexual violation but also objectification of the victim—treating a child as a sexual being with words or actions or permitting others to do so.

Spiritual abuse comes not from sharing with your children what you believe but instead putting them in untenable organizations such as cults or permitting them either directly or passively to be abused in some other manner—sexual, physical, emotional, or verbal—by someone in a role of spiritual leader.

Psychological abuse involves manipulation and control of the victim.

Verbal abuse is name calling, demeaning, yelling, threatening, or scaring to gain control.

Emotional abuse is blaming and shaming the child for things over which they have no control, neglect, or abandonment.

Abuse creates lifelong impact not only on those who are directly victimized but also on those who witness the abuse and those who have relationships with the victims later in life. This is called secondary abuse.

Secondary abuse leaves psychological scars that can be severe. For example, there are families in which one child becomes the target of parental abuse while the other siblings are not directly abused but are forced by proximity or intent of the abuser to see or hear the maltreatment of the target child.

The witnesses have conflicted feelings—grateful not to be the target, guilt for feeling grateful, fearful of becoming the target, frightened of what they are seeing and hearing, and, perhaps most important, powerlessness to stop or change what's going on and shame at not being able to change the outcome. The targeted child may be somewhat protected by the siblings or, in some families, almost pushed forward to the perpetrator parent in an effort to protect the witnesses. In either case, the siblings' relationships are damaged for life.

People who experience abuse, primary or secondary, often suffer from posttraumatic stress disorder (PTSD), which is the result of experiencing or witnessing a life-threatening or life-ending event. You can think of PTSD as a built-in warning system. With PTSD, the brain stores life-threatening or life-ending experiences with many cross-references. Primitive humans needed to have this enhanced warning system to be able to survive the perils of life. An encounter with a saber-toothed tiger would be stored not just as scary but with cross-references to the five senses as well as the time of day and year, the environment, the location, and the weather. The early humans who best used the benefit of PTSD were the people who survived to make more people. As a consequence, the genetic components of PTSD have come down to us.

Unfortunately, what started out as a way to preserve our species also makes life difficult for modern survivors. Some people have one PTSD experience—a car accident, a work accident, or some other frightening event—and while it certainly leaves its mark if there's no other event, the original incident becomes woven into the survivor's life story and normalizes.

Conversely, when someone is subjected to repeated assaults or PTSD-inducing experiences, they combine to make the PTSD more complex and difficult for the survivor to overcome.

The symptoms of PTSD include anxiety, rumination (obsessively thinking about the event), avoidance of similar situations, nightmares, flashbacks, intrusive thoughts or memories, irritability, low self-esteem, guilt, shame, hypervigilance, concentration problems, sleep problems, self-destructive behavior, a need for control, or exaggerated startle response. It's a complex disorder and everyone who suffers from it has their own unique constellation of symptoms and triggers.

Triggers are circumstances or situations that bring up the traumatic memories in one way or another. An adult who was abused as a child may not be able to tolerate the sound of a crying child because it accesses those cross-references and brings up the feelings and fears of the abuse experiences. Triggers often produce intrusive thoughts, rumination, flashbacks, or even anger. Those responses can lead to feelings of inadequacy, low self-esteem, or even self-harming or risky behavior. In that way, PTSD behaves like an avalanche tearing through the life of the survivor, even with such a seemingly small thing as a child crying.

In addition to PTSD, survivors of parental abuse often have a lot of trust issues, which makes perfect sense. It is perfectly reasonable for a child to expect a caregiver, especially a parent, to be safe and a refuge from the fears of the world. When that supposedly safe person is the abuser, trust is broken and repeated abuse breaks it again and again. Because there is little possibility of the perpetrator making amends with the child, that broken trust is not likely to be repaired.

As an adult, the survivor may seek relationships and want to be close and trust, but the PTSD and trust issues get in the way and the survivor is likely to flee. Sadly, because the supposedly safe parent perpetrated the abuse, the survivor may be drawn to abusive partners in an attempt to "fix" the abusive parent by proxy. While it may be perfectly obvious to the logical brain this isn't going to work, the survivor's unconscious mind sees this as a potential resolution of the childhood experiences. Therefore, the survivor of childhood abuse remains caught in the abusive patterns and experiences as an adult, increasing his or her PTSD.

You may have noted I initially used the word "victim" to describe the recipient of the abuse but later changed to "survivor." How a person who has suffered abuse describes themselves, internally and externally, is extremely important to their healing process. If you think of yourself as a victim, you have surrendered your power to the abuser and your healing will be more difficult if not impossible. If, however, you call yourself a survivor of abuse, you are taking back your personal power from the perpetrator and setting yourself on a healing path.

The process of healing from childhood abuse by parents or parental figures is not quickly accomplished because it is a complex experience. It is, however, possible and achievable—and hard work.

Start by finding a therapist who has experience working with PTSD and adult survivors of childhood abuse. Your therapist is your partner in healing who will help you learn trust, which is the first step to healing. Without being able to trust, healing is impossible.

A little philosophical aside:
If you trust no one, you trust everyone.

In other words, when you say, "I don't trust anyone," what you are really saying is, "I trust everyone equally." That is a risky position because it means you don't distinguish between people who are safe and people who are dangerous. Without being able to make such a distinction, you put yourself at risk in all relationships. That's why learning to trust is the critical first step in healing.

Working with the therapist will also help you learn to identify and feel your own emotions as well as being able to identify and interpret the emotions of others. Kids who are abused have trouble with emotions because they get confusing information about feelings from the parents who should be teaching them. If the perpetrator says, "I love you," one minute and then is beating you the next, love doesn't make much sense. Hence, you need to learn emotions and their expression.

You will also need to process your abuse. Don't panic: You do this over a long period of time and only as you feel safe to talk about it. You can expect to be uncomfortable. After all, talking about what happened to you and how you felt about it is difficult. The objective is not to relive the abuse but rather to take away its power by exposing it and then to be able to put it in perspective and store it in a safe place. You cannot erase what happened to you, but you can regain power over it rather than it having power over you.

In addition to a private therapist, you may want to find a support group or therapy group of other survivors. Sharing experiences and support with others who have had similar experiences is another way of restoring your personal power over your abuse. It's not for the purpose of comparative abuse—mine or yours was worse—but instead to see that you are not alone and to help you learn compassion, not only for others but for yourself.

Compassion will allow you to forgive yourself. Often survivors of childhood abuse by parents blame themselves for what happened to them as though they somehow deserved how they were treated.

You are not responsible for what happened to you. You were a child who was victimized by someone who should have been the safest person in the world for you.

You did not deserve what happened to you. No child deserves to be abused. For that matter, nobody deserves to be abused. Blaming yourself for the awful behavior of someone who should have known better is a kind of self-abuse and a block to healing.

You are not what happened to you. You are a survivor. This is why you must treat yourself with great compassion and forgive yourself.

Building self-esteem is also part of the healing process. Your abuser treated you like an object rather than a person, and because your abuser was a person you should have been able to trust, you came to believe you were nothing more than an object. This perspective led to your low self-esteem.

You are not an object. You are a person who deserves to be loved and treated with kindness. Your therapist and support group will help you raise your self-esteem and confidence.

Building relationships is also part of healing, particularly with trustworthy partners and with your own children. Part of that process is believing you deserve to be loved by people who are safe and caring. As you learn to trust yourself and others and work through the memories, among your rewards will be strong, happy relationships.

Let's take a minute to talk about teasing. In healthy families, teasing is gentle and a way of showing love. My dad used to call me "Princess Lightfoot Morning Laughter" because I am a heel-first walker so I was noisy, and I wasn't then and am not now a morning person. He always said it with a genuine smile. If I had objected, he would have stopped immediately.

In abusive families, teasing is a form of verbal abuse. It's intended to hurt the target of the teasing; to humiliate them, usually in public, and it's directed at their most vulnerable spots. It's delivered with a sneer, not a smile. If you were teased in your family of origin and it felt like abuse, it was.

Healing from parental abuse is a long process, filled with ups and downs. What happened to you cannot and will not be erased. If you have PTSD, and it's likely you do, it will always be there. The purpose of therapy is to teach you how to manage your history and your PTSD so that it doesn't take over your life. Just keep reminding yourself: *I am a survivor.*

The other part of the healing process is to decide what, if any, relationship you want with your abuser. Some people decide to cut the relationship off completely, and that is certainly an option, particularly if the abuser has made no effort to apologize or change.

If you decide you want to have some relationship with your abuser, you deserve to be the one who sets the expectations and rules for the relationship. You also deserve a sincere apology and a demonstration of changed behavior. Perhaps you might ask your therapist to mediate between you and your abuser to achieve that apology and define the relationship going forward. Don't rush into a reconciliation. Be sure you're ready. Treat yourself with respect. And remember: "No" is a complete sentence.

❧15❧

Absent Parents

A parent or parents may die, divorce, or abandon their families. Work or military service may take a parent away. Electronic communication can help keep distant families connected, a very recent advantage. But if a parent is truly absent from the life of their child, there may be unfinished business, unresolved issues, or unanswered questions. Here's the good news: There are ways to resolve those open wounds.

Carl's biological father has never been present in his life. He and Carl's mom, Becca, had a tempestuous just-out-of-college relationship that ended abruptly when her pregnancy with Carl was revealed. When Carl was five, Becca married Nelson, who then adopted Carl. Unfortunately, Nelson and Carl did not bond, instead often butting heads and arguing.

Nelson reverted to parenting as he had been parented and was often violent with Carl, then justifying his behavior to Becca by claiming Carl needed to be "taught respect." As Carl became an adolescent, their disagreements became mutually violent and Carl left home, living with friends' families until he graduated from high school. He and Becca would meet without Nelson's knowledge and she would give Carl money, but no matter how much he begged, she would not leave Nelson. Carl went to live with Becca's parents, from whom she was estranged, when he started college about 400 miles away from his mother and Nelson.

Carl was in his junior year at college when Becca told him she was divorcing Nelson. Almost immediately, Nelson began to communicate with Carl, presenting a very different memory set than Carl recalled about their early relationship. Nelson talked about his fond memories of their fishing trips as Carl recalled the one time they had gone fishing with Nelson and his dad and how both men had yelled at him and berated him. He reminded Carl he'd never missed one of Carl's sports events, and Carl remembered Nelson lecturing him after games and events about how badly he'd played.

Carl had finally become frustrated with Nelson's distorted stories and confronted him. Nelson responded with anger and defensiveness, finally saying, "You're not my son. You've never been my son. I only adopted you because I wanted your mom."

Carl came to therapy carrying the burden of abandonment by both his biological father and his adopted father as well as the estrangement with his mother. While they had reconciled after Becca's divorce, Carl still believed she had chosen Nelson over him and Becca hadn't wanted to discuss it.

As we worked together, Carl was able to see the effects these three major abandonments had in his life. He had major trust issues and had never had a relationship or friendship that lasted more than about three months. He also recognized how much he isolated from people in general. In addition, Carl admitted he had anger management problems.

"I go from calm to irrationally furious in a nanosecond. It's worst when I'm driving and someone does something I think is stupid. I will scream at them and sometimes tailgate them or even consider running them into a ditch. It takes a long time for me to calm down and then I am embarrassed by my behavior, but it's far too late to apologize or correct myself. I'm sure I've scared people. Hell, I scare myself."

We made the anger management a priority by looking at how his anger was related to the abandonment issues by both father figures. "My best father figure has been my grandfather, Arnold. At first I was afraid to trust him because my mom has major issues with him, but as I lived with them while I was in college, I saw how much he really cared and how strong and steady he was. I learned a lot from him but not how to maintain a relationship or control my anger."

I asked Carl to write his two fathers and his mother letters about the impact their choices had on his life. I assured him he would never mail them but urged him to be honest in his feelings and to say what was in his heart to each of them. It took over a month for him to finish the first letter. He'd chosen Nelson and the letter was filled with anger and recriminations. We spent time talking about the incidents in the letter, then I asked him to write a letter to himself as Nelson, apologizing for and owning all the behaviors and incidents about which he had written to Nelson. His Nelson-to-Carl letter was powerful for Carl as he finally "heard" the words of apology and kindness he'd needed all his life. We did the same with his biological father and his mother.

One day Carl came into a session grinning. "I think I crossed a major bridge today. I was able to have a road incident without losing my mind. I got a little irate, but I didn't yell and I didn't do anything stupid. I talked myself off the ledge. It was like I was watching myself from a distance and the adult in me was in charge."

That day was pivotal in Carl's recovery work. The letters had been a strong agent for change for him and laid the groundwork for his moment of revelation, but what turned the corner for him was being able to apply the theoretical in real life and succeed.

Carl's situation with several layers of abandonment by significant adults is more extreme than some, but his work is typical of what needs to happen in order to heal from an absent parent's abuse or abandonment.

Abandonment can be experienced by a child if the parent is living or deceased. If the parent has died and things were left unresolved or unaddressed, it's important to work through, even in their absence, because unresolved issues are still issues. They may be minor, in which case you can probably address them on your own using the letter technique Carl used. Don't be surprised if resolving something, even something minor, brings up feelings. That's the point. You want to be able to address the issue, bring up the feelings around it, and then put it away. Once you have felt the feelings and looked at the issue from the perspective of resolution rather than reworking, you'll be able to think about it with less emotional baggage and put it away.

If, however, there are a lot of unresolved or unaddressed problems, you will want to work with a therapist who can help you by guiding you through one issue at a time. When I talk about this with my clients I cite the example of a balloon. If you blow up a balloon, don't tie off the neck, and then let it go, what happens? Right, it flies around the room unpredictably and might seem to chase you or attack you.

If, however, you blow up the balloon and hold onto the neck with both thumbs and index fingers, then pull the neck apart a little bit, what does the balloon do? Right, it deflates slowly while making a squeaky whistle but it remains in control. Therapy is squeaking the balloon but keeping it in control.

You don't want all your feelings to come up at the same time. It would be overwhelming and scary. One memory and the attached feelings let you feel what you need to feel without feeling scared or out of control. Working on one thing at a time lets you see it, feel it, process it, and put it away. Only when you have done those steps are you ready to move on to the next issue. Carl needed to work through his "layers" in a controlled environment where he felt safe.

When working through issues with parents who have passed, you also have the additional layer of grief to deal with. Losing a parent, even one with whom you have major issues, is a milestone in a person's life and has a profound effect. Grief at this seminal loss can extend for a lifetime. At first, it's acute and comes with a lot of raw feelings, but over time grief becomes more subtle. Reminders of events, good and bad, can raise surprising sadness and discomfort. You may seek out reminders of the absent parent even if they are upsetting. Some people will revise their history with that parent, making it "better" in order to resolve the unfinished business.

Honesty, however, is the best policy. Rarely is a parent so bad there are no good memories. Looking only at the good memories is two-dimensional just as much as looking only at the bad memories. Your parent was a three-dimensional person and deserves to be remembered in three dimensions. This is not to say their negative behavior was acceptable, but rather to encourage you to see them as whole people, warts and all. When you are able to do that, it's far easier for you to keep them in perspective; to honor the good stuff; and to, eventually, forgive and understand the bad behavior. Nobody is perfect. Nobody is perfectly evil.

We tend to ascribe only negative feelings to people who have treated us badly and positive feelings to people who have treated us well. It's emotional shorthand. "Dad was mean to me most of the time so he was always mean," or "Mom was so patient and loving and was so good to me. She was the perfect mom." The truth—and you know this in your heart and soul—is Dad and Mom were both human. Dad had his soft, gentle moments and Mom had her bad days, but it's usually easier just to lump them into one category—mean or wonderful—for storage and reference.

Seeing people as two-dimensional may be more efficient for storage and reactive purposes but the truth is it's unfair. It's unfair to them, and ultimately it's unfair to you. There is, of course, a caveat. There are rarely those people who are genuinely to-their-core evil and those who are in the same way good. Parents who wantonly abuse their children or torture or sell or odiously neglect them fall into the to-their-core-evil classification and have no place in the lives of those children. That sort of toxicity should never be forgiven and that relationship should absolutely be abandoned.

Other than those toxic relationships, make the effort to see the multidimensional nature of your parents. Maybe there is some event or influence in their lives that caused them to make the choices they made. Perhaps there are things that went on in their lives that you, as the child, were not privy to. Understanding adds dimension and lessens the burden of anger and negativity you carry.

Forgiveness of someone who has never apologized nor asked for your compassion can be difficult, and it's why Carl's letter writing was effective. In his first letter, from Carl to his absent parent, he was able to vent, to express the anger and pain he had felt, to connect the feelings to the events. This is important to the process of clearing up old business because it's very hard to let go of something you're holding onto very tightly. Getting it out in the open, saying it, writing it, acknowledging it, feeling it lets you also control it, manage it, and put it away.

The second step of writing a letter of apology and acknowledgment of negative behavior is equally important. Even though you know intellectually these words are not coming from the problem parent, your inner child who felt the pain of those angry words or physical violence hears/reads/ listens to those expressions of kindness and remorse and begins to heal.

Inner child? John Bradshaw, a psychologist and writer, published a lot of work about healing the inner child. Briefly, his hypothesis was that each of us carries remnants of our damaged child-self with us as we grow into adults. When we encounter situations that bring forward feelings those parts of ourselves experienced, those inner children emerge, bringing with them their unresolved pain.

I remember as an adult having what at the time seemed like completely out-of-proportion anger with my mom when she broke a promise she had made. When I brought my behavior up with my therapist she asked me how old I felt when I was so angry. Before I could even think about it, I responded, "Nine." She then asked me to close my eyes and focus on the nine-year-old inner me.

As I relaxed, I remembered a similar incident with a broken promise when I was nine. Not only did I remember but I also felt my feelings of frustration and betrayal at the time. My therapist then encouraged me to reassure my inner nine-year-old she was safe and I, now the adult, would keep her safe and we would figure out a different solution to the current problem. Which I did. The conversations with my inner nine-year-old helped me let go of my exaggerated reaction and look at my mom's reasoning from an adult perspective. Once I did so, it was easy for me to see her view and find a different solution.

Dr. Bradshaw's work with healing the inner child is very powerful and very approachable. You'll find his book in the bibliography at the end of this book. It's work you can do on your own or with a therapist, and it can be very effective at getting to resolution.

If the absent or abandoning parent is willing, it is also possible to resolve those difficult issues face-to-face. I strongly suggest you have a neutral mediator—a therapist—involved in this process. This is absolutely the time to squeak the balloon and not try to fix everything in one session. It would also be important to be sure you are in a place emotionally where you feel strong and as though you have your issues addressed before you begin to meet. And if you feel the meetings are not productive or are harmful, you have the right and the power to say no and end the meetings.

You deserve to have resolution on issues with absent parents. There are a number of ways to get that resolution, but as you do the hard work, keep reminding yourself you deserve resolution. Because you do.

16

Toxic Parents

Sadly, there are some parents who are not only incompetent or distant or absent but genuinely toxic for their children. These parents commit extreme abuse; have extreme addictions; are criminal; belong to cults or gangs; have serious and persistent mental illness; traffic or criminally neglect their children. They express no remorse and take no responsibility for their choices.

Sally came to my office while she was in the process of divorcing Jack, her husband of almost thirty years. "I don't know why I waited so long. All four of our kids are adults. He's been working all over the country for the last few years so I guess I just put it on the back burner—until he came home last summer and I found out he was living in another city with a woman he'd met at his last consulting job. He told me he was in love with her. That finally motivated me."

Sally went on to explain that Jack had cheated on her openly throughout their marriage. "He was so charming and he always promised it would be the last time and I believed him. I have no idea why. But then the kids started coming, and I was a stay-at-home mom. Which I loved. My kids are the best."

Her two sons and two daughters are all very successful and well-educated. The oldest is twenty-eight and an executive at a major corporation, and the youngest is twenty-two and in medical school getting a dual MD/PhD. Sally has a job in an office she likes. "I never finished college. Jack got his PhD and had always told me as soon as he finished I could go back but that, like practically everything else he said, was a lie. He ran up over $150,000 in student loans and then told me I had to get a job to pay them. And I did."

We worked together a long time to figure out why she did what she did throughout the relationship, and it turned out to be Jack's sociopathy and ability to manipulate and her willingness to believe him because she thought she loved him and he loved her. Part of her tenacity in the relationship was from fear. Jack had been physically, emotionally, psychologically, and sexually abusive toward her.

She still fears him. Although Jack doesn't know where she lives, he knows where she works. Statistics tell us the second largest cause of death for women in the workplace is murder, most often by an intimate or former intimate partner. As much as she likes her job, she is looking for a different one for her own safety.

"If I get killed, please make sure they go after him," she says she has told her mom and her friends. A sociopath falls under the Antisocial Personality Disorder diagnosis on Axis II that we talked about in Chapter 12. Sociopaths are relentlessly charming and social. The problem arises from their complete lack of compassion or empathy or remorse. Sociopaths operate from a gratification perspective: what they want is the only thing that matters.

Jack, with his glib charm and manipulative skills, has no friends other than the woman he's living with, in part because he has borrowed money from all his previous friends and never made any effort to repay it, even though his consulting business has been successful. He has not made any effort to repay his student loans and has significant tax problems.

"He's Teflon," Sally said with great frustration. "Any regular person would be in prison for even one of the things he's done. Meanwhile, the IRS writes me letters but not him. He's stolen from friends and nobody presses charges. He's years behind in student loans, and they don't go after him. I just don't get it."

All four of Jack's children have completely rejected him and cut him out of their lives—the boys because he took money from both of their bank accounts without their knowledge or consent, and the girls because he sexually abused both of them when they were prekindergarten age.

The eldest daughter, a successful executive at twenty-eight, remembered what happened with her father when she was meditating just after graduating from college. She immediately went to therapy to work through her memories and the issues that arose when she remembered the abuse. When she felt confident after several years of working with her therapist, she confronted Jack. He laughed in her face.

Her sister, third in line, began having nightmares about the abuse incidents right after her freshman year in college. She shared her nightmares with Sally and agreed to see the same therapist as her older sister. She would like to confront Jack, but wants nothing to do with him. She also takes into consideration what he did when her older sister confronted him.

Jack's father—once a well-regarded corporate executive, according to Sally—is now in prison. He was convicted of being a serial rapist, with many victims in the same cities as several of his corporate offices. He will be in prison for the rest of his life. Jack's mother believes he was wrongly convicted and has a number of restraining orders against her for stalking and harassing victims who testified against him as well as several female members of the jury.

Two of Jack's four brothers have repeatedly been through drug and alcohol treatment and live with their mother. The other two brothers are estranged from the family and have been for many years. Sally told me she is regularly harassed by her former mother-in-law, who refuses to believe Jack could be a predator like his father and can't believe Sally would divorce him.

Jack continues to contact all four kids via text and email but none of them respond. They are all very loyal to Sally and very supportive of her. Jack also wrote many abusive emails to Sally until she deactivated all the email accounts he knew and changed her phone number shortly after their divorce was final.

"I am finally free of him," she said one day in a session. "I feel like I could fly if I wanted to. I'm light as a bird. I'm free. I haven't seen an abusive email in three weeks and when my phone rings, I know it's someone I want to talk to. All I need now is a new job and I'll feel completely safe. After almost thirty years."

Jack and, for that matter, his parents are perfect examples of toxic parents. All four kids and Sally have made the correct choice to cut off the relationship with him. He continues to be abusive even at a distance.

Remember: The only way to win with a narcissist or a sociopath is *not to engage*!

THE TRULY TOXIC— CONS, CROOKS, AND KILLERS

Unfortunately, there are people in the world who are truly dangerous to the rest of us, particularly to their children. We've talked about narcissists, sociopaths, and psychopaths in the chapter on mental illness, and some things bear repeating when we discuss toxic parents.

It's important to embrace the reality that you will probably never understand why these people do what they do. Frankly, that's good news because narcissists, sociopaths, and psychopaths do not operate from the same set of rules as the rest of society. If you don't understand them, it means you don't think like they do. Narcissists, sociopaths, and psychopaths see the world from a strictly intellectual perspective. If emotion is present, it is usually a mimic of what they believe emotion is, and they are using it to manipulate us to do what they want us to do.

The total goal of these toxic people is to get what they want. They don't care what it costs you or how you are impacted. All they care about is winning. For them to win, you need to lose. There is no middle ground. And if you engage, you will lose because you come equipped with what to their minds are fatal flaws: compassion and empathy.

Empathy is the ability to put yourself into the emotional position of another person. Your friend calls sobbing because she has had to make the hard decision to put her beloved dog to sleep. Your eyes fill with tears and you feel that same panicky/sad/anxious twist in your gut you know she's feeling. You can't fix it or change it, but what you can do is feel it, and in doing so, you give her emotional support.

The narcissist, sociopath, or psychopath may say something that sounds like, "I'm really sorry," but they don't feel it. Instead, they will be trying to think of a way to turn your emotions to their advantage. Maybe you will need "comforting" later so that they can take advantage of your weakened emotional state, so they direct the conversation to how they can get what they want. Your feelings, your needs, and your fears don't even cross their minds.

Narcissists, sociopaths, and psychopaths are sometimes hard to tell apart. They are all self-focused, all manipulative, all liars, all entitled, all grandiose, and all believe they are special and above the rules of society. All three groups require a great deal of admiration from others but give little to anyone else except to make themselves look better. The lack of empathy or compassion is vivid in all three. The differences arise in terms of criminal activity or motivation and degree.

Narcissists believe they are above the rules of society but are not as likely to be involved in openly criminal enterprises. They may speed, drink and drive, and cheat on their spouses and taxes, but they generally are not openly criminal. Narcissists are less likely to maintain a charming persona. Instead, they are initially charming until they think they have you "hooked," and then they embark on a program of tearing you down and demeaning you so that they can control you.

The message of the narcissist is you will never be "good enough" to be anything but disappointing to them. The ultimate result of this sort of battering is the victim goes into autopilot and badgers themselves into trying to be perfect while assuring themselves they will never make the grade. The victim wants to be loved and keeps trying to be "good enough" to regain the initial charm of the narcissist, believing that charm to be the reward for perfection.

Narcissistic parents may overpraise their young children, then become hypercritical as the child grows older, focusing on the child's achievements rather than the personality and "whoness." The message is clear: You are only of value for what you can do, and can do to make the parent look good, not who you are.

Sociopaths, on the other hand, tend to maintain their charming personality to connect with others, but it is not authentic, caring charm. Instead, it is a carefully refined manipulation designed to weaken your defenses so that they can take advantage of you. Sociopaths are very similar to narcissists, except that sociopaths have criminal intent in their charm. Sociopaths are the con men and women, the people who knowingly take advantage of others, devoid of remorse or empathy. Sociopaths connect with others only to take advantage of them in one way or another. There is no emotion, only the illusion of emotion, masked with charm. Their motivation is always to win, but unlike the abuse of the narcissist, sociopaths make you think their winning was your idea in the first place.

Sociopathic parents charm their children while using them for their own purposes. The kids believe the charming parent to be authentic until they figure out at some point how they have been conned, but by then the sociopath has presented their charming façade to everyone surrounding the children so the kids end up looking resentful and angry rather than victimized.

Psychopaths, as we discussed before, occupy both prisons and executive suites. Their cardinal trait is the absolute absence of compassion or empathy with little or no attempt to conceal their contempt for those they consider to be inferior to them—a group that includes the vast majority of the world. We are but game pieces in their lives. They make up the rules they live by and, if challenged, blame others for not being smart or clever enough to understand them. They manipulate others according to the rules they make up and then disdain the ones they manipulate.

People use the word "psychopath" interchangeably with "crazy" because of the rules variability, but true psychopaths are calculating, manipulative, cold, contemptuous, and remorseless. They are dangerously devoid of emotion. Some—generally those in nonprison environments—can maintain a social façade, but if you watch them you can see the façade has an element of theatricality. They know it's fake, and they don't really care if you know it's fake.

Psychopathic parents are the most dangerous of all because of their lack of connection or even willingness to try to connect. Their children are objects and they are used like objects. It would be impossible for the child to live up to anything they may imagine is demanded of them because the psychopath's rules won't make sense. So the child tries to be what the psychopathic parent wants—but that parent doesn't care, so nothing will ever be good enough. The child grows up without guideposts or rules that make any sense and ends up a rudderless, disempowered adult, likely to follow in the path of the psychopathic parent.

I can't stress that enough. Narcissists and sociopaths—and their extreme versions, psychopaths—do not think like the rest of the world. Their whole process of reasoning isn't even close to what the majority of people use. When you engage with them, they perceive you as a combatant, and they will focus their energy on your destruction so they can "win." They don't care what you need or what you want. They have no empathy or compassion and see these traits as weaknesses in others to be exploited for their benefit. They actually enjoy watching you be uncomfortable or upset and may provoke you "for fun." The only technique that will work is absolute and complete silence and lack of engagement.

"The limit of your self-abuse is the limit you will tolerate from other people. Nobody hurts us worse than ourselves, therefore we make the rules up about how we are to be treated, and what we think we deserve based on the wounds we learned growing up."

—Don Miguel Ruiz

ELEVEN WARNING SIGNS
OF TOXIC PARENTS

Toxicity, like dysfunction, tends to seem to be unique in each person. However, there are some general elements that will show themselves in virtually all toxic parents.

1. *You are the problem.* Toxic parents are unable or unwilling to own any part of the problems they may have created. Instead, you are told repeatedly if you were only better, richer, prettier, smarter, taller, or thinner, there would be no issue. Toxic parents are so externally focused they are unable to see they have any part of the problem.

2. *Controlling behavior.* Parents who need to control your every move once you are an adult see you as their property and that you must be compliant with their every demand.

3. *No boundaries.* Because they have no boundaries themselves, toxic parents will ignore any boundaries you try to establish and often be angry or vengeful when you attempt to establish yourself as a separate entity. People without boundaries believe they have the right to do anything they wish because they don't see where they stop and you begin. It's more ownership than relationship.

4. *Violence or abuse.* There is never a justification for violence in a relationship for any reason, no matter what. Period. The only exception would be self-defense and even then violence should be the behavior of last resort. There is no excuse, explanation, rationalization, clarification, or justification for interpersonal violence. The same is true of abuse of any sort: verbal, emotional, financial, sexual, psychological, or religious. Violence and abuse create very unbalanced relationships. If you are the child of a violent or abusive parent, you are in a toxic situation.

5. *Conning or criminal behavior.* If your parent or parents are engaged in criminal activity, you could find yourself under suspicion even if you are not involved. If you are being conned by a parent or have

been victim of their criminal behavior, the hardest but best thing to do is to involve law enforcement. It will protect you and likely end the toxic relationship, but ending should be your objective. In no case should you get in any deeper in hopes of recovering what you have lost.

6. *Addictions.* If a parent is unable or unwilling to break an addiction to drugs and alcohol after repeated attempts on your part to get help for them, their message is clear: The addiction is more important to them than the relationship with you. Their addiction is toxic to you.

7. *Put-downs, insults, "teasing."* This is certainly a matter of degree, particularly with teasing. Some families tease, which sometimes can cross the line into abuse. The toxic version, however, is intended to make you feel badly about yourself and to put you in a one-down position so that your toxic parent can feel superior. Remember, these are typical techniques of narcissists particularly. If you have set boundaries, been clear, used appropriate language, and repeatedly asked for these behaviors to stop and they have not, you have a clear indication of toxicity.

8. *Black-and-white thinking.* The inability to be flexible can be an indicator of toxicity. If your parent is unable or unwilling to see anything other than absolutes—something is either right or wrong, good or bad, yes or no—she will also be unwilling to give you any room to make mistakes before you are condemned as being completely wrong and therefore bad. This is not good for your self-esteem and mental health.

9. *Yes, but . . .* If you hear more excuses than explanations and apologies, and if every, even slight, confrontation is deflected with, "Yes, but . . . ," you are dealing with a parent who is unwilling to own his or her behavior. This parent is looking for someone to blame, and you are likely to be that person.

10. *Double binds.* A double bind is a situation in which, no matter what you do, you will be wrong. Everyone experiences some double binds

in relationships and in life. For example, you hate your job, but if you quit you won't have any money. Parents who consistently put you into a double bind are trying to keep you off balance and take your personal power away. Disempowerment is toxic long term.

11. *Lying.* I'm not talking about the little social lies everyone tells about small things, but rather the sort of lies toxic people tell to manipulate you and others. For parent(s) who are manipulative liars, it will be impossible to build any trust or reliability with them. Too many lies over too long a time are toxic.

None of these signs are stand-alone indicators that you may want to consider limiting or ending the relationship with your parents, but if there are more check marks, you want to take a long look at the cost of the relationship to you.

If you are the child of a sociopath, psychopath, or toxic narcissist, you may feel you don't have the right to reject them and cut off contact. You have been taught to be blindly loyal to them. It's what they need because, without victims, they can't be perpetrators. They need our cooperation to be able to hurt us. When we stop cooperating, they lose their power.

At first when you cut off contact, you might feel awful, as though you have done something terrible—as though you are a failure at family. You might even reengage or even apologize to the perpetrator. He will then do something to revictimize you, reminding you why you cut him off in the first place. As time goes along and you begin to work through your feelings and issues with the perpetrator, you will feel less and less as though you are the problem and be able to see more clearly who is.

What's hard is when one parent is the perpetrator and the other is not, but they are still together. In essence, the nonperpetrator parent is still a victim who has not chosen to cut off contact. Family functions—weddings, graduations, holidays, funerals—become emotional minefields.

At that point you have to make a plan. If you decide to attend, you can still avoid or ignore the perpetrator. You can limit your time at the event or you can choose not to attend at all. The "victim" parent will object and be sad or mad, but you will be spared contact with your perpetrator, which is extremely important to your recovery. You can make plans with the "victim" parent when the perpetrator isn't present. Or you can ask the rest of the family if they cannot include the perpetrator. Know it is your right to be protected and for others to respect your decision. Always have an emergency exit plan and use it if you need to.

So how do you proceed to make the decision to cut off contact? First, *be ready*. You need to feel strong and certain. Don't be tricked by your hopes of what might have been but rather focus clearly on what is. Work with a therapist so that you are prepared.

Second, *give it a try*. Be less engaged and see how that feels. If you find you are more relaxed, less overwhelmed, sleep better, have fewer or no nightmares, or are happier, then your decision to cut off contact is reinforced.

Third, *expect reactions from the rest of the family when you pull away*. There may not be any support for your decision, or the family may split. Remind yourself you are making this decision for your own mental health and for the benefit of your children. The perpetrator may try to contact you, as Jack did with his children, fluctuating between trying to charm them and railing against Sally as a "bad mother, bad wife, bad person." You can reassure your nonperpetrator family you don't need them to take sides and welcome them to be in contact with you, but without either including or passing information to the perpetrator. Remember, every person walks on their own path and in their own timing. What's right for you at a particular moment may not be what your brother or sister is ready for.

Fourth, *boundaries, boundaries, boundaries*. "No" is a complete sentence. You owe it to yourself to stay strong. Be clear why you are doing what you are doing and that it is a final decision. You will probably be guilted and maybe even abused by those who have not made the same choice, but keep your boundaries intact.

Fifth, *find new, healthy friends*. We call this a "family of creation." You know those friends who you're close to from the beginning. I have a client who has walked away from her family of origin because of abuse. Through her church family, she has made healthy connections with people who support her and encourage her, as she does them.

Finally, *embrace your freedom without being either a crusader or smug.* Both will turn off nonperpetrator family members and new friends. Instead, create your new life and enjoy it. It will speak for you.

17

Stepparents,
Grandparents, and In-Laws

Obviously not all families remain intact, given the slightly more than 50 percent divorce rate. As a consequence, dysfunctional or abusive parents often bring their children into another relationship with its own difficulties and relationship issues. These newly created families may introduce new step- or half-siblings as well as step-relatives such as step-grandparents. Sometimes these blended families do splendidly well, expanding the circle of support and love for the children involved. Some, not so much.

Stepparents, particularly stepmothers, have received some bad press in books and films over the years. This is probably related to the perceived role of mothers as caregivers, and when that dynamic goes awry it becomes grist for the mill of the stories. Stepfathers haven't been as targeted. The truth is, a stepparent of either gender can be dysfunctional and can have a negative impact on children just as they can also be a moderating or safe and protective influence.

Rick was born during the time his father was serving in the army in Vietnam. Rick's mother, Danielle, was mentally ill and abandoned him at the hospital. His dad, Herm, was unable to return to the United States to retrieve him from the hospital, which wouldn't release him to any other family member, had anyone in his father's family been willing or able to take him, which they were not. Rick told me he spent his first eighteen months in the hospital, tended to by nurses where he learned to walk and talk but not to bond.

He was almost nineteen months old when his father was finally able to claim him, but their lives were not smooth. Rick was used to rotating relationships. Herm had no idea how to take care of Rick and turned to his sister, Monica, who had six kids of her own and a husband, Buck, who was an over-the-road trucker, often absent. Rick and Herm moved in with Monica, Buck, and the kids and she grudgingly cared for Rick while Herm worked an overnight shift and slept most of the day but there was still no bonding. Herm couldn't find Danielle, so he was granted an annulment of his marriage.

Then Herm met Kim at work. Kim professed to love kids, and they were soon married. Rick was almost three, and he remembered Kim playing with him when Herm was around but then ignoring him when they were alone. "I didn't care. She was just one more stranger who hung around."

Soon Kim was pregnant, and by the time Rick was five, he had a baby half-brother, Mike. Kim focused her loving attention on Mike, who was quickly followed by Luke. "I was pretty much on my own after the two boys came. I went to school and did well but didn't have friends until I discovered a group of other outcasts in about sixth grade. By that time, Kim had begun using me as the scapegoat. No matter what the boys did, I was to blame and I got punished."

Rick described being locked in a closet or the basement or outside in the winter for hours, being spanked with a wooden spoon or a belt for minor infractions of Kim's ever-changing rules or for no reason at all other than she was in a bad mood, and often going to bed without eating because of something Mike and Luke had done.

Herm wouldn't stand up for him. "I think he was afraid of her, too. He would just sit silently when she wailed on me or screamed at me. He wouldn't even let me in the house on a frigid night when she had locked me out when I was about ten. I slept in the garage more than one winter night, and it wasn't a heated garage."

I asked him if there was anyone he had bonded with besides his other outsider friends. "My grandmother, Herm's mother. She lived in the next town, about fourteen miles away, and more than once I hitched or rode my bike over there when Kim locked me out. Gran had MS and over the years I watched her deteriorate, but she made it very clear she loved me and supported me. Kim would call and demand to know if I was there and Gran would tell her I was and she would come and get me and yell at me all the way home, but I didn't care. I could tune her out by then. When I was fifteen, I went to live with Gran and finish high school. Kim didn't want to take care of her, but I did. Gran hung on until two weeks after I graduated from high school. She left the house to me. Kim was furious."

Certainly not all or even most stepparents are as cold as Kim. I use Rick's story as a vivid example, but I hear many stories from clients in which their experiences with stepparents have been negative or a battleground. Sometimes the child is used as a messenger between the parents who are estranged and the stepparent becomes the mediator. Other times the stepparent doesn't understand that their role is not to replace the mother or father but rather to enhance the child's experience in both families. There are parents who punish or even abuse their children in order to punish their ex or the stepparent.

If you find yourself in such a situation, you need tight boundaries and great communication skills. It's important to be able to clearly and firmly set your boundaries and be clear. In Rick's case, removing himself from the relationship was the smart thing to do, since he and Kim would never forgive one another, understandably. In cases where the stepparent is not abusive or toxic, using relationship management tools (see Chapter 18 as well as Chapter 3) will help you maintain a healthy connection with your biological parent and stepparent.

Not surprisingly, Rick had never married. His longest relationship was about six months. "I know Gran wanted me to get married and settle down, but that's not for me. I like being alone. My dad died three years ago and I went to the funeral, but when I went to sit with Kim and the boys, she had me thrown out." He shrugged. "I haven't had any contact with any of them since, but that's fine."

Rick's story is an example of what happens to a child who is not able to bond appropriately with a parent. He had come to therapy because he wanted to figure out how to feel about his biological mother, his dad, and his stepmother. We did a lot of talking about the concepts of attachment theory.

ATTACHMENT THEORY

The three most prominent early researchers in attachment theory were Dr. John Bowlby in the United Kingdom, whose work focused on the effect of separation on children's development; Dr. Harry Harlow at the University of Wisconsin–Madison, who looked at attachment in primates with his famous—or infamous—experiments with a wire "mother" who gave food and a "soft" mother to see to which infant and young monkeys were attracted; and Dr. Mary Ainsworth at the University of Texas who studied attachment in human babies.

Dr. Ainsworth's work focused on a group of mothers and their one-year-old babies. In her experiment, the mothers and babies were brought into a room where they could be observed through one-way mirrors. The room had a chair, sometimes two, in the center of the room where the mom would sit. The outside edges of the room were ringed with toys. The mom would sit in the chair and put the baby on the floor. After a predetermined amount of time, the mom would leave the room, then return after a short interval. Sometimes the mom would be joined by another woman, a stranger to the child. When the mother left, the stranger would remain. Dr. Ainsworth and her fellow researchers observed hundreds of these interactions.

Dr. Ainsworth identified three types of babies: the first type she called "securely attached." This type of baby explored the room in a daisy pattern, going out to the toys and back to Mom, then out to the toys and returning to Mom again. When the mom would leave, the securely attached child would cry until she returned, be comforted by her, and then go back to exploring.

These kids were judged to have a belief they would not be hurt or abandoned by significant adults. They trusted the adults in their world. Dr. Ainsworth reported that about 25 percent of the babies they studied were securely attached. As adults, securely attached people make secure relationships with their spouses and their kids. Their relationships are characterized by love, good communication, trust, and predictability. In short, they are emotionally available.

The second group of babies in the experiment were characterized by Dr. Ainsworth as "insecurely attached." These babies would cling to the mom and ignore the toys. When the mom left, they were inconsolable. If there was a stranger present who offered comfort to the baby, her efforts were rejected. When the mom returned, however, the baby would angrily reject her and, while still crying, cling to the stranger almost as revenge on Mom for leaving.

Dr. Ainsworth reported about 50 percent of the babies fell into this category. Unfortunately, these children grow up to be insecurely attached adults, alternately clinging to their partners and children, then rejecting them. They may trust the wrong people or flip their trust back and forth between people. They fear being abandoned and might be jealous or clingy in relationships. This group makes up a lot of dysfunctional parents.

The third group of Dr. Ainsworth's babies were characterized as "unattached." As you might imagine, this 25 percent didn't care if Mom stayed or left, their attention totally focused on the toys. When mom held them, they arched away from contact with her. Rick would definitely fall into the unattached group. Unattached kids grow up to be unattached or unattachable adults. They don't value or encourage relationships, and my guess would be that a lot of unattached kids grow up to be narcissistic, sociopathic, or psychopathic.

Dr. Ainsworth said the first few days of life are critical to attachment style. There is some influence from the personalities of the mom and baby, particularly if the mom doesn't trust herself to be a good mom or is herself unattached. Babies are the ultimate narcissists, but they are also instinctively very aware of that first connection or lack of it.

So is the message of Dr. Ainsworth's work that only 25 percent of the population will ever be emotionally available? No, because people can and do learn, grow, and change. Many insecurely attached kids work through their issues and move forward. Rick is a good example. He proved he was able to care with his grandmother, who was the only really loving person in his life. Sadly, when she died, he despaired of finding someone else to love him but was curious to understand his feelings, which he eventually did.

The unattached children have the most work to do to overcome their early-life experiences. Interestingly, while the image of an unattached mom might arise in our brains as someone who uses drugs or is neglectful, unattached kids can also arise from children who are raised by nannies or in day care. Certainly not all, since many children who have other-than-parent care growing up are fine. The early lack of bonding, however, plus extensive other-than-parent care from early infancy can make lack of attachment a real problem. People who are not bonded—unattached—often operate from intellect rather than emotion, have little or no empathy or compassion, and because they don't incorporate feelings into human interactions, are capable of horrific behavior. It's one way sociopaths and psychopaths arise.

Rick began his life as unattached, then learned about love and compassion from his grandmother. He is typical of the vast majority of unattached people who go through life alone, not trusting their own abilities to make long-term, meaningful relationships. The sociopath/psychopath group—fortunately for all of us—is a relatively small subset. Small, but influential.

GRANDPARENTS

I have heard more than one person observe about their parent or parents who have become grandparents, sometimes with humor and sometimes with frustration, "Where was this person when I was growing up?"

The role of grandparent is very different from that of parent. They can be much more indulgent with their grands than they were with their kids. If, however, the grandparent was an unattached parent, such a pattern might persist but not always. Sometimes as people age, their skill sets improve. Without the daily stresses of parenting plus trying to earn a living, maintain a relationship, and survive, the unattached parent can focus their time and energy on the grandchildren. The same is true of insecurely attached parents who become loving, caring grandparents who lose the insecurities they had when they were younger and become thoughtful and caring.

As the child of these "converted" parents, you look on with a combination of wonder, mystification, and some resentment. While understandable, your best reaction choice might better be gratitude for the connection your children have with their grands.

GRANDPARENTS IN THE ROLE OF PARENTS

In other situations, grandparents may be called upon to take on the role of parent with a grandchild or grandchildren. This changes the dynamic of the relationship dramatically. Now the grandparent can no longer be the indulgent, always-loving figure but has to revert to the role of parental duties and the attendant pressures.

When grandparents take on the role of parent, it's also confusing for the child and can create a sense of abandonment by the mom and dad. No matter how dysfunctional a family is, kids assume all families are like theirs until they are exposed to other families where the dynamics are different. This doesn't usually occur until the mid-elementary years when they begin to spend time at friends' homes, sometimes even later.

If the child is turned over to grandparents to be raised before this awareness occurs, the child has no way to explain the abandonment and will often blame it on themselves. Then if Mom or Dad or both come back into the picture for visits and leave again, the child's belief in his or her responsibility is reinforced. "I must be a really awful kid for them to not want me again."

In an effort to avoid further abandonment, children will not be likely to share their concerns with the grandparent(s) and continue to believe they don't deserve to be loved or happy. It doesn't matter how loving and supportive the grandparent(s) are, the child will feel unlovable to some degree. In adulthood this expresses as low self-esteem.

In Chapter 19 we talk more about increasing self-esteem. Obviously low self-esteem arises from more than this one cause and there are kids who are raised by grandparent(s) whose self-esteem is strong, but if you have low self-worth and were raised by grandparent(s), you might examine this idea as a possible source and let yourself off the hook. This process will take time and therapy, but both are a worthy investment.

Kids need to clearly understand circumstances in which there is a dramatic change in their lives—divorce, sent to live with relatives or foster families, abused, whatever happens in the adult world—*the child is not responsible for what has happened.* It's best if this information comes from the parent or parents, but if not, it needs to come from an adult—and more than once.

Sadly, sometimes life with the grandparent(s) isn't much or any of an improvement. These persons may have been the parents who raised the dysfunctional parent who's abandoning the child. They may still be using drugs or alcohol, violent, angry, criminal, or neglectful. This keeps the child in the same emotional place they were with the parents and does real damage.

If you are an adult who's been raised by a grandparent(s) who was as dysfunctional as your parents, you still have the power to change and grow and move beyond your less-than-ideal childhood. You would benefit from therapy with a professional who understands attachment theories as well as who can help you with your self-esteem, boundaries, communication skills, and other tools for change. Don't settle for the damage.

IN-LAWS

When you marry into a family, you marry into their "stuff." Sometimes that's wonderful as you acquire a new parent or parents who are loving and caring and who enhance your life. If that's your situation, you can skip this section.

Unfortunately, it can also mean you might acquire issues you haven't encountered before and will need to learn to deal with them on the fly. If you're not used to dysfunction or to your new family's particular kind of dysfunction, the learning curve is steep.

Marsha came from a loving, connected family. When she met Otto they connected immediately, but he seemed determined to keep her away from his family. She later told me that was fine with her because it meant they spent more time with her family. She met his family briefly at their engagement party because they left before she had a chance to get to know them, making the excuse they had a long drive to get home for their dogs.

The next time Marsha encountered them was at the groom's dinner the night before her and Otto's wedding. Marsha told me she almost didn't go through with the wedding because of their behavior that night. Her future brother-in-law got drunk and got into a fight in the parking lot. Otto's father hit on the waitress, the female bartender, and a group of about twenty-five-year-old women in the bar. Otto's mother sat by herself and refused to speak to anyone other than Otto's sister who loudly proclaimed Marsha to be "trailer trash" within earshot of Marsha's family.

"It turned out their behavior at the groom's dinner was just the warm-up for the wedding. They turned up in jeans and T-shirts, except for Otto's mom, who wore a white gown that looked like a prom dress. I think she was drunk, but it was hard to tell because she wouldn't talk to anyone again at the reception. Otto's dad and brother got really drunk and crashed another wedding reception at the venue, then got into a fight in the lobby when they were ejected. Otto's sister's husband wore a T-shirt that had an obscenity on it. Fortunately Otto was able to get him to change into a shirt Otto had brought, but he relentlessly pursued two of my bridesmaids, then shouted they were 'whores' when they rebuffed him. It was a nightmare. Otto finally made them all leave right after dinner. We didn't see them for several years, much to my relief, but they do show up, usually unannounced, every so often. They don't have anything to do with our kids, for which I am grateful, but I know it hurts Otto since they lavish attention on his brother's and sister's kids."

Marsha has learned coping skills to manage their visits by spending a short time with his family, then taking herself and her kids to run errands or go to a movie while Otto visits with his family. He texts her when they have left so that she and the kids can return. Otto reports his family has never questioned her behavior or asked why the kids go with her.

If you have married into chaos like Marsha, absenting yourself from the situation is an option, but be sure your spouse understands your choice and supports it. Remember, your spouse is accustomed to their parents' behavior and has had a long time to develop coping skills. You don't want him or her to see your absence as a personal affront or abandonment, so communicate your feelings and your plan clearly and be sure you are heard and their agreement is firm.

With milder but still difficult in-laws, make sure your coping tools are fair and agreeable to your partner. Those people might be odd or boring or boorish, but they are your partner's parents. You can ask your partner to limit contact, but there will be times you have to be around them. Be respectful, keep your boundaries tight, use good communication skills, and remind yourself they will go home at some time.

FOSTER FAMILIES

Kids end up in foster care for any number of reasons, usually none of them happy. Sometimes the stays are short, as the biological parent or parents get themselves together. Other times the foster-care system becomes the child's life until they are legally adults and on their own.

Some foster-care families are wonderful and loving and truly enhance the life of the child. Sadly, the system is overloaded and in high demand, and foster families function more as warehouses for kids who get passed from foster home to foster home without making connections. When they emerge from the system as adults or have run away one too many times, they become independent without the skills and emotions they need to effectively survive in the real world. They may be street smart, but are not reality skilled.

If you grew up in foster care, it is critical you find a way to learn how to live in society and function as an independent, emotionally available, and connected adult. Find a therapist. Look for a mentor. Seek a family of creation that wants the best for you in a healthy way. Learn to love yourself.

You deserve a better life than you started with.

PART THREE

Making It Work

18

Relationship Skills and Dynamics

Relationship dynamics are the ways in which families interact with one another, including the power balance and power struggles, emotional connections and disconnections, family traditions and rules, abuse of any kind, finances, alliances and enmities, and the myriad of other interactions and factors inside a family.

Like any other endeavor, identifying and working with family and relationship dynamics require skills. In this chapter we take a look at some of the skills and perspectives that will be helpful in your quest to manage and understand the dynamics in your family. The more you know—the more comfortable you are with yourself and your skills—the more likely you are to be successful in your attempts to manage situations with difficult and emotionally unavailable parents.

CONTROL

We have explored emotion basics and emotional location. Relationship dynamics is where you can apply them to figure out what's going on in your family of origin, particularly with your parents. Understanding your parents' emotional locations and your own—Solver, I hope—and those of your other family members gives you some insight into how your family dynamics work and have worked in the past. Having that insight enables you to develop a strategy to manage yourself in the context of your family.

Self-Management

The next time you're out in public, choose a stranger and, using only the power of your mind and no words or gestures, make them do something. Remember, no words or gestures. Now try the same thing with your spouse or kids or friends or parents. No words or gestures; just make them do something using only the power of your thoughts. How'd that work out? The lesson here is the only person over whom you have control is you.

Remembering you can't control anyone but yourself helps you let go of any attempt to control your way out of a difficult situation with your parent or parents. Your only option is managing yourself.

Certainly one way to accomplish that is to stay in the Solver spot, seeking a working solution to an actual problem. Dysfunctional dynamics will try to pull you out of the Solver spot and into one of the outlying locations where you lose your power. Keeping your power is essential in dealing with problem family dynamics.

Of course, having and keeping good boundaries is another absolutely necessary component. In a perfect world, when your problem parent(s) know your boundaries cannot be violated and understand you will not be brought into chaos, you will be keeping your power. We don't live in a perfect world, so don't assume this means they won't try to entice you to revert to old patterns. People really don't like change, and when you change to be in charge of yourself and have good boundaries and keep your power, you will be upsetting and changing the family relationship dynamic, and they will fight it.

There can be disruption without change,
but there can be no change without disruption.

People don't change until and unless they become uncomfortable enough that change will make them less uncomfortable. Everybody's threshold of ultimate discomfort is different. Some people are able to tolerate a lot of discomfort before they consider doing something differently. Others who are less rigid approach change with less fear and need for control and move more easily into a different position. The more dysfunctional the family relationship dynamic, the less they will be amenable to change.

In our normal, imperfect world you will be under a lot of pressure to loosen your boundaries and abdicate your power so that they will not be disrupted by the changes you are making. Once you decide to let yourself be uncomfortable enough to change your own life, you don't want to have to go through that discomfort again, so you must be strong and resist the pressure.

VICTIM/PERPETRATOR/RESCUER DYNAMIC

Unhealthy relationships among three people often—maybe always—end up in triangulation where two will align themselves against the third. We can all recognize it in middle school friendships, but it's equally common in family relationship dynamics when one or both or several parents/step-parents/in-laws participate.

In addition to ganging up, there is also a more complex version of this negative behavior: the perpetrator/victim/rescuer dynamic. Here's how it works:

Perpetrator ➤ Victim ➤ Rescuer

The perpetrator initiates the contact by attacking the victim. The victim then turns to the rescuer for help, and the rescuer attacks the perpetrator, trying to help the victim. And then everything shifts and the perpetrator becomes the victim, the victim has to take the role of rescuer, and the rescuer becomes the perpetrator.

This dynamic is very typical in abusive families but can occur in any relationship. It has no Solver features at all and is based on finding someone to be wrong or bad or the problem.

To avoid or escape the perpetrator/victim/rescuer dynamic, stay firmly in the Solver spot and do not allow yourself to be sucked into this dysfunctional vortex. Remember, you accomplish that goal by inviting others to join you in identifying the problem and working together to find a solution. If you don't get cooperation, don't get involved. Step away. Make your boundaries clear. Use good communication skills. Say "no" and mean it.

THE IDENTIFIED PATIENT

I'm sure you've heard the old joke: Every family, group of friends, and office has a weirdo. If you can't figure out who that is, it's probably you.

There is a similar concept in family dynamics, but it's no laughing matter. I'm talking about the identified patient (IP). In a family the IP is the person with the physical, mental, or behavioral difficulty or difficulties around whom the family can talk, problem solve, commiserate, blame, and feel superior.

The IP gives the family a rallying point but not usually in a healthy or constructive way. Rather, the family says, "Crazy Bob. He owes everyone in the family money and now he's coming around with some get-rich-quick scheme again. Just be warned, he's going to call you. I already told him no and he got really huffy with me." Eye roll. Everyone in the extended family knows Bob and his backstory, not to mention his diagnosis and a litany of Bob-is-causing-trouble-again stories, which are retold at all small and large family gatherings. Bob is the guy who, when he shows up at a family gathering, is carefully watched and almost expected to act out in some way. He's the family drunk or druggie.

Bob is the guy who's been married five or six times, sometimes without benefit of a prior divorce or two. He's the man who is most likely to ask for money, make a scene, manipulate Grandma and Grandpa or his siblings or their kids or his kids, need bail money, go bankrupt, disappear for months or years, or be incarcerated. Bob takes the family's heat so nobody else has to, even though they may be in similar trouble. Every generation has a Bob.

If Bob or Bobette is your parent, you are well aware of the effects of being the identified patient not only in your immediate family but also in your extended family. Relatives might expect you to be able to control the affected parent. They may also criticize you for not "doing enough" for that parent, as though you have the financial and emotional resources to make a difference. Sometimes you're even seen as part of the problem and are therefore shunned or excluded. Meanwhile, you're on the front lines with a parent who's unpredictable, difficult, and broke.

This is where your good boundaries come into play. You know what to expect from Bob or Bobette's behavior and you can set up your limits accordingly. It's very much okay to say no to requests you can't or won't help with. You are not obligated to bring them into your home to stay or even to visit nor to support their habits. You do not have to invest in their get-rich-quick schemes nor make apologies for their outbursts. You are not responsible for their behavior or choices either with them or extended family.

Remember: "No" is a complete sentence!

THE GRAY ZONE

Parents who are emotionally unavailable have usually lost touch with or never had a connection with their emotions. Generally this starts in childhood, but there is research demonstrating that women who have grown up in a family where there are healthy emotional connections and no trauma who get into an abusive relationship can, after as little time as six months, appear to be as emotionally impaired as a woman who grew up with abuse. The study was focused on women, which is why men are not mentioned.

When we are little, we experience emotions in a sort of sine wave pattern: a little up, a little down, then up again, then a little down again. There are the moments of more intensity that spike up or down, but most of life is within a medium-sized wave. At that time in our lives we also believe our parents are perfect, even if they're not. If you are the child of an emotionally unavailable parent and you're feeling excited, you might be told, "Calm down and stop acting like a fool." If you're feeling sad, you might be told, "Big boys or girls don't cry." Using kid logic, you say, "I must be wrong or bad because Mom or Dad says I'm doing this wrong and I shouldn't feel my feelings."

Experiences accumulate and soon the child has decided his or her emotional cues are all wrong and stops trusting them. Thus, the Gray Zone begins—an emotional area of dense fog into which the person puts all subtle, smaller, daily emotions, not feeling them because he or she has learned not to trust them. Instead, what they experience is only the big spiky highs or the deep canyon lows. No love, only passion. No irritation, only rage. No sadness, only despair.

If you have a parent who is emotionally flat one minute and then blows up the next with a response that seems completely out of proportion to the situation, you may be dealing with someone who has a Gray Zone problem. The emotional roller coaster of the Gray Zone makes it very difficult to connect.

Subtle fluctuations of emotional life are lost to them in the fog they've installed. They don't trust *their* emotions, so they don't trust yours. It's emotionally draining to be around someone who is always either flying or crashing because it's impossible to predict where that Gray Zone parent will be at any time around any issue. You avoid asking for emotional input or starting an emotion-based conversation because you fear the possible response.

Let me quickly add here that I'm not talking about bipolar disorder in any of its forms. The mood fluctuations of people who are bipolar—also called manic depression—are not as mercurial as Gray Zone people. Persons with bipolar disorder generally have a wide sine wave of mood, congruent with their disorder: either manic, depressed, or in transition. These cycles generally occur over a relatively long period of time—weeks or months— rather than hours or minutes.

To the Gray Zone parent, your subtle changes of emotion may be invisible or seen as manipulative or dishonest because he or she doesn't have the ability to read your emotions and consequently predict your behavior or even interpret changes. Instead, the Gray Zone parent will try to provoke an exaggerated emotional response from you so that they can recognize it and you emotionally. They want you to come join them in the peaks where they can "see" you. Suddenly you find yourself yelling at the top of your lungs over something minor, but they are feeling comfortable because they can recognize your emotional state and their own and they feel connected. Meanwhile, you're very uncomfortable.

My mentor and friend Judith Barnitt suggested a novel solution. When you first have contact with your Gray Zone parent, you initiate an escalation into the spikes. "Mom, did you pay for that haircut?" "Dad, are you sure you should spend that money?" You don't want to escalate too high, but you want to jump up into the spikes. They will feel you emotionally and then can attach. Oddly, it does work.

Just don't stick around in the spikes. Once they have connected, you can go back to where you're comfortable because the emotional connection will have been made. Keep your boundaries tight, communicate clearly and otherwise respectfully, and if they continue to try to drag you back into the spikes, limit your visit. You get to be in charge of your own comfort level.

Clients have also had success explaining the Gray Zone to Gray Zone parents. While they may not be able to completely recognize and own their Gray Zone style, even a little understanding of how you experience their spikes can help. If you decide to share the information, do so using "I feel" language so that they don't feel attacked and be certain they see this as constructive. How to accomplish that? Ask.

REFRAMING

Just what it sounds like, *reframing*, the process of moving an idea or emotion into a different form, helps someone open up emotionally, which promotes emotional availability. It's a great way to break a communication logjam by helping the other person feel supported rather than attacked. If you have a favorite old picture in an unattractive frame, you can change the frame.

Here's how it works. The position a person takes in a conversation, discussion, or argument is a snapshot of his or her perspective. That snapshot is enclosed in a frame that changes from one situation to another. The objective of reframing is to change the focus in the situation to a more positive, while still truthful, view.

Let me give you an example. Your mom has been taking piano lessons and has a recital. She's nervous, and so are you. She glances to the audience, then freezes and forgets a major part of her piece, and you find her in tears backstage. You say, "Mom, you gave it a great shot. You'll be fantastic by next year's recital." That's reframing. You don't have to tell her she was awful—she knows. You also shouldn't pretend she was great—she wasn't. By reframing, you have offered support and encouragement without being either phony or condescending.

In other words, reframing is finding a different way to look at a situation without sugarcoating or harshness. In any circumstance where people have very different views, reframing can prove another way to resolve the differences. With emotionally unavailable parents, reframing can provide a safe perspective for them to look at their snapshot. A reframe can allow everyone to win and feel respected.

THE FORBIDDEN WHY

"Why" is usually an attacking word, unless you're four and it's your go-to question about everything. Otherwise, "Why" is usually followed by the (sometimes) unspoken "the hell," as in "Why the hell would you . . . ?" and accompanied by the (sometimes) invisible shaking finger of shame. It's accusatory and tends to put people on the defensive, which makes it a terrible tool for resolving conflict and creating healthy communication.

When I work with couples, forbidding them from asking "why" is one of my first steps because it's a blame gateway. People sometimes use "why" as though an explanation is a solution to a problem, as though knowing *why* someone made a particular choice will somehow make the pain or anger or sadness go away and will therefore solve the problem. Nothing will change simply because the motivation for an action has been explained, particularly if it feels like a judgment has been made in advance.

"Why" is gratification-focused rather than solution-focused. "Why" seeks someone to be wrong so that the other can be right, putting the other communicator in a one-down position and the asker feeling superior. "Why" also shifts focus away from positive emotional connections as the askee struggles to explain that which may be unexplainable or might make the situation more complicated since often a person's motive is nonlinear.

"Why" also allows an emotionally unavailable person to stay in his or her head and out of touch with themselves emotionally, which permits and fosters emotional unavailability. Explanations are brain-based, while understanding is emotion-based.

So what to say instead? My favorite is "Help me understand. . . ." Do not follow that open phrase with the forbidden "why." Instead, say, "Help me understand your decision process when you . . ." If you read that out loud, I suspect you'll immediately see the difference between "Why" and "Help me understand." You're not asking for an intellectual explanation but rather an understanding of the process of coming to a particular decision.

Another useful replacement for "why" is "I wonder. . . ." Again, don't follow that useful question with "why" or you'll defeat your purpose in making the change. Instead, you could say, "I wonder if you thought of a different solution such as . . ." It's another way of making a suggestion for an alternative outcome without sounding aggressive or judgmental. All you're doing is wondering. It opens the door to a discussion with everyone joined in the Solver spot.

"Help me understand" and "I wonder" are both very useful in emotionally charged situations. You can use either or both not only with your difficult parents but also with your own kids. "Help me understand your decision to skip school/quit football/take the car without permission/not do your homework." When you ask for understanding of motivation, you might still get the "I dunno" answer, but do not settle for that phrase. Ask again. Kids recognize a nonaccusatory approach as being nonthreatening, and you might actually open a dialog.

Parents get it, too. "Mom, help me understand your process to decide to take a cruise rather than pay your mortgage." Although your internal questioner may be screaming "Why," at the top of its lungs, you want to keep the door open to solutions and understanding rather than just a gateway to blame and fighting.

BUT ...

Another word you may want to avoid is "but" because "but" erases everything that came before it. "Mom, you really planned the party well, _but_ you didn't get the invitations out in time." You have complimented her and retracted the compliment in the same sentence. That's passive-aggressive.

Instead of linking the two sentences with "but," break them apart. "Mom you really planned the party well. I'm sorry more people didn't come. Perhaps next time you could send the invitations out earlier so that people can plan around it." With the small change, you have preserved the compliment and made the suggestion without erasing anything.

Part of getting what you want in a relationship is to demonstrate how you would like to be treated and spoken to. Getting the relationship you want with your emotionally unavailable parent(s) benefits from demonstration of your ability to behave differently in the context of the relationship.

AN INTERNAL FEEDBACK SYSTEM

As we looked at earlier, we talk about an internal locus of control and an external locus of control. Those phrases refer to having and developing an internal feedback system to help you make decisions.

Having an internal locus of control means you have the tools and experience to make a good decision without seeking, or with seeking very limited, input from others. Obviously if you are engaging in something you've not encountered before, you will ask an expert for input.

Let me give you an example. My brother is the head computer guy in a school system. He knows so much about electronics and computers that when I need input about a particular program or piece of hardware, I ask him. Then I use the information he gives me to help make my decision. The decision is still mine, but I've consulted an expert.

External locus of control means a person looks outside him- or herself to establish how to react or what to choose. External locus is typical of adolescents as they are all trying to be different by being exactly the same as their peer group. It's certainly something, in its most extreme, street gangs count on. It's also something girls who go shopping together do. "It's so cute on you" reinforces the adolescent buyer's decision and makes her feel part of the crowd, both important to adolescents.

External locus of control also operates with emotionally unavailable parents who look to you or their friends to make important decisions for them rather than taking the risk to make the decisions for themselves. This falls into the realm of what we used to call passive-aggressive behavior. That diagnosis is now included in Narcissistic Personality Disorder, but the behavior is the same.

Here's an example. Your dad wants to buy a car. He knows your mom will object to his choice so he calls you. "Son, you know so much about cars. I want a new car." You notice he doesn't ask you directly to help him. Instead, his approach is passive-aggressive. His objective is for you to make the decision about what car he buys, so that when Mom explodes, you are at fault.

Instead of falling for the passive-aggressive bait, say, "Dad, help me understand what you need from me." You are asking him, in a nonthreatening way, to be more direct with you. You might follow up with, "I wonder what car Mom wants? Have you spoken to her about it?" With those two phrases, you are getting yourself off the hook and out of the line of fire and putting Dad back in charge of his own decisions.

The development of an internal feedback system provides a blueprint for emotional responses. To develop an internal feedback system you need to begin by taking the risk to consult with yourself first. Ask yourself, *Do I know enough about _____ to make this decision?* Start small. At the grocery store thinking about what to make for dinner, don't phone your partner. Instead, use your internal wisdom. What would you like to eat? What did you have last night? What have you had lately that was deli-cious? Obviously, you don't choose something someone else won't or can't eat, but you make the decision based on your own knowledge and internal process. As you practice, move on to bigger decisions. As you develop trust with yourself and learn to identify your own and others' feelings using the basics—mad, glad, sad, and scared—you will feel more confident about mak-ing your own choices.

I "FEEL" LANGUAGE

When you want to communicate emotional content, a really effective technique is to use "I feel" language. "Mom, I feel sad that you and I don't have better communication." "Dad, I feel mad when you put me in the middle of an argument you're having with Mom."

From the examples above, you can see the form. Here it is broken down into steps for your convenience.

1. *Begin with the person's name or title.* People pay better attention when they hear their name or title. It's why higher-pressure salespeople say your name all the time when they're trying to sell you something.

2. *Then say, "I feel," followed by the name of the feeling.* If you're dealing with someone who's emotionally unavailable, use one of the basic four feelings—mad, glad, sad, or scared. Don't confuse "I feel" and "I think." Often people say "I feel" when they mean "I think." The test is, can you put the name of a feeling in the sentence?

   For example, "I feel you are being a jerk," has no emotion or feel-ing in it. Hence, it's an "I think." The feeling version would be, "I feel mad that you are being a jerk," though that's not a very supportive approach to getting what you want. Instead you might want to try, "I feel sad when you and I don't have better communication."

3. Then *explain succinctly what you are feeling the emotion about*, as I did in the above last sentence.

4. Then *stop and allow the other person to respond.* In a perfect world, the person will say, "I hear you say you feel sad that you and I don't

have better communication," opening the door for you to affirm and then offer suggestions for how your sadness can be remedied. One step at a time.

If you get to Step 4, you have achieved what's called "reflective listening," a major tool in conflict resolution and a skill to model in response. Because it's not a perfect world, Mom might respond, "I don't feel we have poor communication." You may have noticed Mom responded with what is really an "I think" meaning she wasn't engaging emotionally.

Then you can reply, "Mom, I would like to talk about how we can better communicate with each other using feelings." Your response returns the conversation to the emotional realm. "May I make some suggestions?" I am hopeful you will then have opened a dialog in which you can help Mom recognize her feelings ... and yours. Don't give up. You will likely feel frustrated and you can express your frustration using "I feel" language. Eventually, you will succeed if you stick with it.

Remember to breathe!

CONFRONTATION

I know. You *hate* confrontation and will do anything you can to avoid it. Unfortunately, those feelings are probably part of your relationship with your emotionally unavailable parents because people who are emotionally unavailable will go to great lengths to avoid confrontation, as it demands an emotional presence.

Don't confuse confrontation with aggression. Confrontation can and should be quiet, focused, and assertive, not angry or aggressive. It's important to keep emotional location in mind when you need to confront someone. Occupy the Solver spot and invite the parent you must confront to join you in problem solving.

First, use "I feel" language. Rather than the aggressive, finger-pointing, "You are the problem," approach of the Blamer, start with an "I feel" statement. "Mom, I feel glad about your wonderful relationship with Henry. I want to remind you we've asked you not to give him soda or candy because we're trying to keep his sweet tooth under control. I know you want him to know how much you love him. Please do that with affection or attention rather than sweets."

Second, you'll notice I used the sandwich technique—compliment, confront, compliment—along with the "I feel" statement. It's an effective tool to use during a confrontation—as it helps you stay away from the land mines of an aggressive approach.

Third, remember the old saying: "You catch more flies with honey than with vinegar." You are much more likely to be heard and get cooperation by using the gentle confrontation approach of "I feel" language plus the sandwich technique. Generally people don't absorb negative confrontations well, and resentments are created that prevent further healing.

Since you don't like confrontation, using the softer approach may make it easier for you to follow through to set your boundaries and get the outcomes you seek. You might even feel less uncomfortable with confrontation.

THE THREE-SENTENCE RULE
GOAL SETTING

An important part of connecting with emotionally unavailable parents is to set goals for your relationship. Since it is unlikely they will spontaneously change or recognize the dysfunction of the relationship, it will be up to you to set goals.

Goals are best when they have several qualities:

1. *One objective.* You want to make a goal achievable and measurable, so keep it simple. "My goal is to call Mom at least once a week for the next month. I will do that by putting a call reminder on my calendar."
2. *Timeline.* You notice in the goal example above there is a timeline for achievement.
3. *Plan.* Again, in the example above, you have outlined a plan to achieve your goal.

Once you have achieved your first goal, set another.

Goals can be short-term, medium-term, or long-term. Short-term goals are a week or less; medium-term goals can be up to a year; long-term goals can be up to lifetime goals. Generally, relationship goals will be short- or medium-term. And they might stretch into long-term, depending upon the difficulties inherent in the relationship you're working on or, conversely, the success they achieve.

The best tools are the ones that work. You might need to try a lot of different approaches before you find the answer. Don't be discouraged if something doesn't work or doesn't work right away. The problems in your relationship with your parent(s) didn't happen overnight; they won't be resolved overnight.

Breathe. Deeply and often.

19

Getting Rid of Expectations, Guilt, Resentment, and Regrets

The four problems listed in the title are traps making a mess of our relationships. Traps prevent us from emerging into healthy relationships and keep us stuck in old, dysfunctional patterns. So now—since you've learned about feelings and mindsets, emotional location, communication skills, magic words, trust, boundaries, body language, relationship dynamics, and related skills—you don't want to move backward in your progress. Let's look at ways to unload these traps.

EXPECTATIONS

Relationships are easily damaged by unmatched and unmet expectations. We expect our parents to love and care for us in the optimum way— whatever that means—and when we figure out their actions didn't always match our expectations, we have feelings, some of which might be anger or sadness or anxiety or all of them and more. Expectations are kinds of wishes for how we would like the world to be, how we would like our families to be, and how we would like our parents to be. Frequently we start our expectation building in childhood. Some of these expectations take the form of,

"When I grow up, I want to be a _____, just like my dad [or mom]," and for some people the childhood expectation becomes a goal and, eventually, a career. Other people leave the dream of being a cowboy or a fairy princess or a flying dinosaur and move on to careers in which they can find actual jobs. Over time, our expectations grow, particularly as we observe other families and watch movies and TV shows and read.

Expectations often lead to disappointment. Of course there are people who set the expectations bar so low, or so negatively, for friends and family that their expectations are met. If your parents are toxic, addicted, seriously mentally ill, personality disordered, or abusive, it's probably reasonable to set your expectations for them low, particularly if you're trying to build the relationship. High expectations, on the other hand, are often hard to meet because sometimes the expectations are more hopes and wishes than grounded in reality. It's the difference between possible and probable.

Possible vs. Probable

Spread your arms wide, even with your shoulders. This represents the scope of *possible*. Almost anything is possible: zombie apocalypse, winning the lottery, being kidnapped by aliens, becoming a movie star. The possible is virtually infinite.

Now move your arms forward until your hands are about six inches apart. This represents the scope of *probable* and helps us eliminate the unlikely, such as zombie invasions or hitting the lottery for huge money. The probable is practical and realistic. Expectations are best when they fall into the realm of probable.

When you set expectations for others, you must consider not what's possible but rather what's probable. Ask yourself, *Am I hoping Mom will stop being so negative or do I really believe she can make such a challenging change?* When you examine your expectations in the light of possible versus probable, you're likely to adjust your expectation to achievable reality.

A realistic expectation allows you to set goals. Remember, goals need to be measurable, realistic, and one subject at a time. Goals are the action that drives the idea of the expectation.

"I'm going to schedule a time with Mom to talk with her in a gentle and supportive way about Grandmother's negative views of the world. I will not bring up her negative attitude at this meeting as my goal is for her to talk about her mother's negativity and how it makes her feel."

Of course, there is the other side to expectations, and it is expectations others set for you. In healthy families and relationships, those expectations are usually shared and reasonable. "Carlos, you know our family believes in education, so even though you are just going into middle school, we hope you will focus on good grades and school activities so that you will be able to get into the best college possible. We will support you in any way we can." That's a long-range, healthy expectation. It's clear and detailed and includes a guarantee of support by the family.

The insidious expectations in unhealthy families are different. First, they are often unspoken until you have violated them. Second, the consequences of the violation come in the form of criticism, frequently expressed either in front of others or to others who then relay it or spread it, depending on your relationship with the hearer. In either case, you find yourself the unwitting center of unflattering attention for something you didn't know you were expected to know or do or be. Third, the unspoken and unknown expectations then make you edgy because you don't know what other traps are out there waiting to grab you. What you do know is they are there.

Hidden expectations shred trust and self-esteem. Being publicly chastised for disappointing your parents is humiliating, and if your letdown of your parents is a story spread far and wide throughout the family and friends, you begin to want to avoid your parents and their messengers, which functions to isolate you, making you a further target of criticism and commentary.

A permutation of unspoken expectations is what I think of as second-hand praise. This occurs when you hear through the grapevine that Mom has been telling all her friends how successful you are while one to one you are the target of criticism. She tells other people how special you are for two reasons: One, it makes her look really good to her friends to have such a successful child, and two, it "will give you a big ego" if you are praised directly. The effect it has on you is a combination of pride and sadness, and you're not sure which feeling to trust.

Ultimately, hidden expectations are damaging to your self-confidence and create self-doubt. How can you trust your internal feedback loop that tells you you're successful when someone who should be your biggest cheerleader is critical to your face and behind your back and then suddenly switches gears and tells others how well you're doing? It's unsettling.

The answer is having a strong enough internal feedback system and trust in yourself so that you can overcome the critical ambushes or confusing praise. "That's just how Mom operates. I feel confident in myself and my skills," is the way to manage the stealth attacks and praise. Don't let either get you down or up.

When you are subjected to public criticism, don't retort or try to counter or argue. Wait until you've calmed down, then use your communication skills to talk with the critical parent. "Mom, I felt really hurt and embarrassed when you criticized me in front of other people. I didn't know you felt disappointed, and I would have preferred to hear your feelings directly and in private." You may not get a perfect response or you may even get a critical response, but you will have demonstrated good communication skills and made your feelings known. And she might just hear you.

GUILT AND SHAME

Guilt is feeling badly about what you do or did. Shame is feeling badly about whom you are. Guilt is a powerful weapon that has been wielded from the beginning of time, I suspect, from parent to child. Used by itself, guilt can be a powerful teacher for kids. When it is coupled with shame, however, guilt is emotionally destructive.

"You're a bad kid, Kevin, because you lied to Dad about your homework."

"I'd be proud of you, Danielle, if only you hadn't ruined our family gathering with your behavior."

Repetitive linking of guilt (bad choice) with shame (bad person) really damages self-esteem in kids. Destroying self-esteem dooms a person to self-doubt, underachieving, self-directed anger, and likely, depression and anxiety.

If you have been guilt/shamed and fit the description as an adult with low self-esteem, the good news is you can change by working on your self-esteem. The place to start that work is to become aware of how you talk to and about yourself. Often people with low self-esteem will put themselves down, internally and publicly, in a joking or not really joking manner ("I'm such a bad cook I gave my cat food poisoning") or directly saying out loud how "bad" they are ("I hope I don't get chosen for this project. I'm just not smart enough to work with the really good people.").

People with low self-esteem take the approach of putting themselves down because they believe they can beat people to the punch who they expect would say the same thing about them. It doesn't occur to them that others may have a completely different and positive view of them. They have learned from their early years that the best defense is a good offense—against themselves.

Once you have begun monitoring how you talk to and about yourself—and it will probably make you cringe, which is a healthy sign you're paying attention—you want to change that dialog. You catch yourself saying, internally, *I know I won't get that promotion. I'm just not good enough.* Rather than letting that stand, replace it with a positive affirmation: *I deserve this promotion, and I will do everything I can to get it.*

**An affirmation is a true and
positive statement about an ideal outcome.**

Affirmations may seem silly or uncomfortable when you first start saying them because you've been carefully taught to feel negatively about yourself, which is why you must use them repeatedly and often until they sound normal and correct. Your negative inner voices will do battle with the affirmations because those voices have been in charge for a long time, so you must commit to confront.

Parallel to saying good things *to* yourself, say good things *about* yourself.

It's not bragging if it's true!

"Mr. Wilkins, I know you're considering a number of candidates for this job. I would like you to know I believe I would be very strong in this position and would be an asset to the department."

You're not bragging. You are making a true and positive statement about your abilities—a public affirmation.

It's a lifelong process, the battle with the guilt/shame voices, but it's worth the work.

RESENTMENT

"Resentment [anger, hatred, rage, etc.] is like drinking poison and expecting someone else to die." This quote and all its permutations have been attributed to many sources, from Aristotle to Augustine of Hippo to Alcoholics Anonymous. It doesn't really matter who said it first or even the form in which it was couched because it's a wise thought. The only person you harm when you harbor feelings of resentment is yourself, not to mention it takes up a lot of mind space that could be better used.

Let me hasten to add, I am *not* advocating "just stuff all your feelings and forget your parents were emotionally unavailable." Such a perspective is the absolute opposite of my recommendations. What I am advocating is for you to let go of resentment and turn that energy to healing.

Resentment and its close cousin, anger, take up a lot of space in your psyche without doing anything to your benefit. Resentments develop when something unjust happens to us and nobody does anything to correct the injustice or apologize. Resentment tends to be cumulative, adding up over time and experience to become a burden.

Obviously, when you're a child you can't confront a parent who is neglectful or abusive without consequences, but as an adult, using good communication skills, good boundaries, and respect, you can talk about your feelings and rid yourself of the resentments you carry.

It's not simple, and you may still not get either acknowledgment or apology, but the benefit of unburdening yourself makes it worth the effort.

Moses initially came into my practice because his wife "dragged him, kicking and screaming," as he said to me at our first meeting. "She says I'm a bundle of resentments."

As we talked, he began to tell me about his relationship with his parents. "They should have been divorced before I was conceived, frankly. They hated each other. The only thing they could unite on was me. And not in a good way. My dad believed in physical punishment from as early as I can remember, like three, and my mom was big on psychological torture. She used my dad as her enforcer. She'd start drinking right after breakfast, and she was a mean, angry drunk so anything I did infuriated her. Then she'd say, 'When your father gets home, you're gonna get it.' And then she'd sit and nod approvingly while my dad beat me."

Moses continued. "I admit I resented both of them, and I will admit as I got older I almost took pleasure in the beatings my dad gave my mom. She finally divorced him when I was eight after he broke her femur with a baseball bat. I was sent to live with my aunt Jalissa and that was the best thing that ever happened to me. She was amazing. Loving, thoughtful, and sober. When my mom tried to take me back, Auntie just shook her head and said, 'Over my dead body.' I remember sitting on the stairs, watching them. Mom was angry-mean drunk and Auntie stood her ground until my mom left. I didn't see her again until I was eighteen when she showed up at my high school graduation with her second husband and their four kids. She had found religion and stopped drinking, but I could feel the meanness still there, right under the veneer. She pretended I had been the problem, and she had to send me to Auntie to protect herself. I haven't seen her since. My dad died from a fight in prison when I was about fourteen. He was doing time for domestic abuse of his third wife."

There is no question Moses had resentments and plenty of reasons for them. His early childhood was a disaster. Sadly, his aunt Jalissa was unable to erase the damage of his early years, but on the other hand, her loving-kindness and sobriety encouraged and nurtured him. He admitted she had tried to get him to go to therapy when he was an adolescent, but "I thought therapy was for crazy people and I wasn't crazy."

I encouraged Moses to write letters to each of his parents, expressing every one of his resentments with them. I told him he wouldn't have to send them in the classical sense of letters but rather use the letters as a way to move his resentments from his brain to written form.

One day he brought in his laptop to show me his progress on the letters. "I'm almost done with both of them. I just want to go back and make sure I've gotten everything out. I feel lighter, better. My wife says I'm different." He was different.

If you find yourself holding resentments that are dragging you down like an anchor, you might want to try the letter writing solution. If you still have contact with your parent(s) you can also try to talk it through with them. I suggest you do it in little steps, not in one big gush. Stick to one incident and its attendant feelings at a time and be prepared to back away if abusive behavior or language appears. Remember, just because you're ready to resolve some old stuff doesn't mean they are.

Do keep in mind that your memories of what happened may not be the same way they recall the situation. If your memories are of early childhood, remember that adults are big people when you're little and your inner child's recollections may have been different because of that size and authority difference. Be prepared to at least hear your parent(s) out, even if they recall something completely different or don't recall anything. You have the right to be heard and your memories and feelings to be acknowledged, as do they. Don't feel you necessarily have to forgive them or accept their stories but do hear them out.

Good boundaries, good communication skills, and low expectations can be your best assets in these conversations. And please keep in mind your objective is to say what you resent and then set it aside by committing it to paper or computer rather than holding it in your brain to poison you. If you get an apology or acknowledgment, consider it a bonus. Clearing it from your brain is the objective.

REGRETS

Regret can be just as toxic to your psyche as resentment. Regrets occupy a lot of memory energy and have the additional burden of providing a source for rumination—that obsessive thinking about something over and over, trying to fix whatever happened or didn't happen by worrying about it. Regretfulness condemns you to living in the past along with the frustration of not being able to change it, no matter how hard you try.

People regret things they didn't do or didn't say. They regret decisions they made or choices they didn't choose. They regret opportunities lost. They regret disappointments.

Regretful people, as we talked about when discussing mindsets, live in the past, and sad is their default emotion. It's not unusual for regretful people to be depressed and isolated because of their rumination and the amount of emotional energy it takes.

Everyone has regrets about something in their lives. It's part of the human condition. If you don't have regrets, it's likely you've never taken risks and have always made safe choices. The difference between having a regret or two (or twenty, for that matter) and being regretful is rumination. Everyone thinks about things they regret once in a while, usually when someone or some event reminds them of the situation they regret, but most are able to shake off the feelings and don't ruminate about them.

If you are the child of dysfunctional parents, you may ruminate about things you experienced—or didn't experience—in your childhood. These losses fuel resentment, and resentment fuels regret and rumination, a terrible spiral to trap you in your past.

You can break the cycle. Step one is, obviously, to recognize how much time you spend ruminating about your regrets. I suspect you'll be surprised how often your brain drifts in that direction and how long you stay there.

Once you have established the amount of time, the second step is to write down the events and feelings you most often ruminate about. For most people, such a list will be at most four or five items long, often less.

Now you have a list, so step three is to write as detailed a description as you possibly can of each event and the associated feelings it brings up for you. Take your time with this step and be thorough. You've been carrying these things around in your head for a very long time and you want to be certain you have them in detail.

Next, when you have written as much as you can, sit down with your notes in a comfortable, safe place. You might want to have a cup of tea or coffee or some lemonade. Then read each entry. Give yourself five minutes to ruminate about each event, then fold the paper carefully, put it in an envelope, and as you seal it, bid it farewell and remind yourself you are glad to see it carefully put away. You will have honored the experience, felt the feelings, allowed one last rumination, and put it away.

You may want to talk to your parents about the regrets in which they are involved before you accomplish the third step if you believe it would be productive for you. You don't have to, and you would want to avoid doing so if it would just stir up more trouble and cause more rumination. You get to be in charge.

At the same time as you are doing all of this, you may want to connect with a therapist who can help you process your experiences and work with you to manage your depression. You deserve to be happy.

You deserve to live in the present. You deserve to let go of things you can't change.

❧20❧

Empower Yourself
to Change

Throughout the previous chapters, we've looked at techniques to manage difficult parents. We've explored some new approaches and different ways to think about these relationships.

In this chapter, we're going to look at approaches and techniques you can employ to empower yourself. Change is difficult. You need motivation, endurance, persistence, determination, and skills. I can give you motivation and skills. The rest is up to you.

Change is hard work, but ask yourself this question: *If I don't choose to change, what are the consequences?* Usually the consequences of choosing to stay in the same place, are you will always get what you always got. You wouldn't be reading this book if you were happy with what you've always gotten. Be strong. Be determined. Be persistent. Open yourself to being different than you were.

F.E.A.R.

One of the primary obstacles to change is fear. Change means doing something differently than you have done it before, which means you won't be an expert as you were with your old behavior. Conventional wisdom says one becomes an expert after 10,000 hours of performing a particular action or skill. I would guess if we added up all the time we spent in dysfunctional or maladaptive approaches to dealing with difficult parents, we'd all be experts, but not in a good way.

Fear tells us scary, negative stories and exaggerates any even slight threats into pending catastrophes. Fear locks us into uncomfortable places by telling us change will be even more uncomfortable. Fear feeds indecision, and indecision fuels fear in a descending spiral designed to keep you immobilized.

A well-used model to remind people of the components of fear is:

F ➤ False
E ➤ Evidence
A ➤ Appearing
R ➤ Real

Fear is a liar. It tells us we have no control over ourselves or our situation. It presents lies as truth and then exaggerates the possible consequences. Fear creates the illusion we have no choice and no power.

Reason conquers fear. You might remember we talked about the difference between *possible* and *probable*. Fear lives in possible. Reason lives in probable.

BREATHING

Another thing that conquers fear is breathing correctly. When we get anxious or fearful, our bodies respond with adrenaline that constricts blood vessels on the skin and dilates them in our legs so we can run, around our lungs to be able to absorb more oxygen, in our brains so that we can think more clearly, and in our arms to be able to fight. Unfortunately, anxiety often makes people breathe more shallowly, dropping the blood's oxygen level. The brain detects the drop and sends out an alarm, increasing our adrenaline levels and, ultimately, leading to more shallow breathing and increasing anxiety.

"Okay," I can hear you saying, "I know how to breathe. I've done it all my life."

Yes, you have. We're just going to refine and improve your techniques.

Belly Breathing

Put your hand on your stomach and take a big, deep breath. Did you feel your tummy move out and then in as you exhaled? That's how we're supposed to breathe all the time. If your belly didn't move but your shoulders and chest did, you're breathing shallowly. Breathe from your belly.

Interestingly, posture also plays a key role in breathing correctly. If you slump, you are effectively reducing your lung volume and not using those resources to their best effect. Your grandmother was right. Keep your back straight and shoulders rolled back. Keep your head squared on your shoulders and your chin up. You will feel the difference not only in your back but also in your breathing.

Slow and Circular

This refinement is to help overcome the rapid, shallow breathing that often accompanies anxiety or fear. Interestingly, when you inhale through your nose it sends a message to your brain that you're calm, whereas when you breathe through your mouth, especially if it's rapidly, your brain interprets this as an alarm and sends out the message for more adrenaline and to prepare for fight or flight.

For this exercise, inhale through your nose for about four seconds. Without pausing, purse your lips as though you were going to whistle, then exhale for eight seconds. Don't pause, and inhale through your nose again. Be sure you're using belly breathing. You should feel your shoulders drop and your anxiety should drop. As you practice, you can increase the inhale to six and the exhale to twelve, or eight and sixteen.

In respiratory therapy, exhaling through your tightened lips is called "pursed lip breathing," and it actually creates kind of a back pressure in your lungs, expanding the little air sacs called alveoli where oxygen is brought into the bloodstream and carbon dioxide is removed to be exhaled. Our lungs are efficiently designed for this exchange process, and keeping all the alveoli working as much as possible is an excellent idea. Cardio exercise accomplishes the same thing.

Intermittent Circular

In this technique, which is very similar to the slow and circular technique, you inhale for six seconds, hold for six seconds, exhale through pursed lips for six seconds, rest for six seconds, and repeat. Be sure you breathe from your belly. This rhythm helps your body stay calm because of the rhythm and belly breathing. It also helps you focus on staying in the present because you have to be "here" to count.

Fear and anxiety want you to live in the future, and according to fear and anxiety, it is the most dangerous and dystopian possible environment filled with scary things that even go bump in the daytime. When you are feeling fearful or anxious, in addition to breathing, you also want to bring yourself into the present—the only time you can influence. You cannot correct that which has happened and you cannot accurately predict and precorrect the future. Being in the present is the power position.

Along with either circular or intermittent circular breathing, you can also use a couple of other techniques. The first one I call touch and say. In this you put your hand on a nearby object and say its name, then move on to the next object, put your hand on it, and say its name: computer keyboard, desk, water bottle, coffee cup, pencil, pen, notepad, phone, chair, and so on. It doesn't take long to bring you out of the past or the future.

The second is similar. In this technique you name five things you can see, four things you can touch, three things you can hear, two things you can smell, and one thing you can taste. You can switch out the order of the senses if you choose. Again, doing this brings you back into the present.

Your Nose Knows

Our nostrils naturally switch from one side open to the other about every thirty to forty-five minutes. (I know you're inhaling through your nose right now to see which side is open, which is totally appropriate.) When we're anxious or fearful, that switching gets out of sync and we get stuck on one side. To reestablish the rhythm and lower your anxiety, close one nostril by pressing from the side with your thumb or index finger. Inhale slowly for about four seconds then, leaving your finger in place, exhale for about eight seconds through pursed lips. Then switch your thumb or index finger to the other nostril and inhale for four seconds, then exhale for eight seconds through pursed lips. You should feel yourself relaxing and find your nasal rhythm re-established.

The great thing about breathing exercises is that you can do them in the middle of a meeting, in a traffic jam, at a movie—any time you feel anxious or fearful or even just to raise the oxygen levels in your blood if you're feeling tired or logy.

COMMUNICATION AND COURAGE

We've talked a lot throughout the book about using more effective communication and confrontation techniques: using "I feel" language, paying attention to your emotional location and that of the person or people with whom you are communicating, using active listening, respectful language, reframing, and more. Each of those approaches requires two things: practice and the courage to speak.

When you're dealing with emotionally unavailable parents, particularly those who have been abusive, the courage to communicate can be very difficult to gather. If you have found in the past that communication or confrontation produces yelling, anger, even violence, it's very hard to talk yourself into speaking up, even though you know it's the right thing to do.

Remember, people don't change unless they are uncomfortable. When you're trying to work up the courage to communicate or confront, you will be uncomfortable with the idea. When the discomfort with the situation you're wanting to address outweighs the discomfort you feel at the thought of the communication or confrontation, you are ready.

A couple of important considerations:

First, start small. If you have an issue with Mom's extreme verbal abuse and demeaning treatment of you, that's too big an issue to take on. Break it down into smaller chunks. When Mom is verbally abusive, what words does she use that really hurt? Choose one of those words to address.

Second, prepare. When you are getting ready to speak to Mom about her put-downs and abuse, planning is essential. You need to choose a situation in which both of you are calm. Write a script and memorize it so that you have a pathway to follow and you're not just blundering about trying to mumble your way through. Use "I feel" language.

"Mom, I feel very sad when you tell me I'm acting like Uncle Mitchell. That comparison hurts my feelings."

Then stop. *Silence is a powerful tool.* Allowing silence to build in a conversation or confrontation lets you keep your power, gives everyone involved time to think through their responses, and hopefully keeps the emotional level manageable for all concerned.

Unfortunately, Mom may respond with something like, "Well you are just like Mitchell. You're not responsible. You jump from one thing to another. You think everyone is interested in what you're doing, and you drink."

The temptation will be, of course, to try to defend against all four attacks in one sentence. Don't. Instead, respond with some form of the following: "Mom, help me understand what you see as me not being responsible." Then stop. You are keeping your power in the exchange by asking for further information, one accusation at a time.

"Well, you know that time in high school when you were late for curfew? And that time when you were in college and you had an incomplete? And then after college you moved to Los Angeles?"

Don't defend. Instead, ask, "Are there other examples?" Keep your tone respectful and conversational.

"Well, I can't think of any right now, but I know there are." Mom has just run out of gas. Don't gloat. Respond.

"Thank you for the examples. I don't see those three things as being a pattern of irresponsibility. I absolutely missed curfew once, but I did call you to let you know I was going to be late. I remember we talked about my being late on the phone and again when I got home and I understood you were upset and apologized. As for the jobs in college, all were server jobs and I stayed with each of the restaurants for the school year each time. As for moving to Los Angeles, I had talked about it at length at the time with you and Dad, and you both agreed it was a good place for me to be if I wanted to be in the entertainment business. Do you remember those conversations?"

Mom may feel like she has to defend herself and you can listen respectfully, but then bring the conversation back to your point. Don't argue. Instead, ask, "Help me understand how you see me jumping from one thing to another." Again, stop. Let her respond.

"When you were in college you had three different jobs. When you moved to Los Angeles, you got a job as a waitress, then went to work for some entertainment agent and then changed agencies."

Again, as for any other examples, don't defend. Use the "other examples" and then follow up with your perspective. "Mom, I can see how you would think those moves might seem like jumping around. You know I didn't move to LA to become a server, so when I got the opportunity at Entertainment Unlimited, I went for it. Then Robin Jones made me a much better financial offer after almost two years with EU, so I took it. I'm still there three years later." And stop.

I think you have the idea. Say what you're feeling, ask for clarification, respond to small pieces, listen, be respectful, don't let yourself be baited into a fight, and let there be silence.

Finally, build on your success. Once you have taken on your first communication/confrontation and feel even a little successful, you will find repeating the experience is easier. Don't cluster the confrontations/conversations. This didn't happen overnight, and it won't be fixed overnight. If you come on too strong or too quickly, Mom will be shocked and might even be mad and shut down. Timing is important. Stay on your path, but remember it's a path, not a racetrack.

CODEPENDENCE

Being codependent is allowing yourself to be used—for money, for drugs, for a punching bag (emotional, physical, or both), for alcohol, for anything a person should be doing for themselves. If you find yourself getting sucked into parents' dramas and pushed to take sides, that's codependence. They are expecting you to pick a side and stick up for them.

Many people walk a fine line between codependence (which is being a Fixer) and helping. The extreme cases are the easiest to identify—the son who finances his parents' drug use because he believes he can control their use through money; the daughter who buys Mom a fifth of alcohol a day to keep her from having seizures; the child who helps the father obtain extra painkillers, citing love as the reason.

The more difficult to spot are the codependents who permit themselves to be used and abused in smaller ways: twenty dollars here and there, permitting verbal abuse, allowing manipulation, making excuses for parents' behaviors. All of these actions are that of being a codependent/fixer and are unhealthy for all concerned.

The most powerful word to deter someone from using you is "no." You don't have to be snippy or angry. Stay in the Solver spot, use good communication skills, seek alternative solutions, have good boundaries, and say "no."

As you remember by now, "no" is a complete sentence.

MINDFULNESS AND MEDITATION

There is a strong movement now toward meditation and mindfulness. The two are linked because meditation is a way to open the door to mindfulness.

Meditation is sitting quietly, eyes open or closed, in a comfortable position and a peaceful space. Gentle music, essential oils or aromatherapy, and comfortable clothes are all good ideas but whatever works best for you is what's best. Begin by breathing in the slow and circular style. Then here's the part that requires lots of practice: empty your mind. If worries or life issues want to come in, just keep them moving right on through.

When you first begin, start small. If you're not used to sitting quietly without outside distractions, five minutes of meditation may feel like forever. Trying to push yourself beyond what you can tolerate will likely discourage you. On day one, you might be able to manage thirty seconds. That's thirty seconds you weren't able to do before. Wherever you are able to begin, practice expanding your time, even if it's just ten seconds a day.

A trick that works for some people is to imagine a white background in your inner theater. Put a black disc in the middle of the background then let it expand until you have a totally black background. Then put a white disc in the middle of the black background and push it out until you have returned to the white background. Try to do this a number of times without letting any other thoughts enter.

Once you have learned how to create and maintain the blank screen, continue to expand your time. You will find as you go along that things will begin to come into your mind not connected with life worries or current events but rather some deeper understanding about yourself or your life. Ultimately, the goal of meditation is to completely clear the mind, leaving it an empty space. At that point you have now become an expert meditator.

Some people find guided meditation to be a good way to start. In *guided meditation*, you will be walked through a meditation experience by a person with a gentle voice and, often, accompanied by soft music. If you go onto the Internet (Google, Yahoo!, YouTube, and many other sites) and search "guided meditation," many resources will pop up. You can choose among specific topics (stress, relaxation, breathing, healing, etc.), length of the meditation, or both. Some meditators use guided meditation exclusively.

What you will find as you meditate is that your anxiety levels drop, you will feel more rested, your mood will improve, you will be calmer, and you will be more able to deal with people at home and at work—and with your difficult parents.

Mindfulness is being present in the immediate moment—also known as being in the now—calmly feeling your emotions, and being present with your feelings. After all, we can't change the past or predict the future. All we have is the little slice of time we are in at the immediate moment. When we approach the now with emotional presence, we are more able to manage both the experience and our feelings about it.

While being mindful sounds simple, it's actually a challenge for a lot of people because we have been trained by society to carefully inspect our past and prepare for our future. Certainly reflection on the past is important, but not if it becomes an obsession and or an attempt to change the reality of the past at the expense of the present. The same is true of the future. There is a fine balance between preparation for the future—education, goals, finances—and trying to manage the future to the degree you lose the now, especially if such preparations lead to anxiety and fear.

Examination and preparation are important, but living life outweighs both. Being present with your feelings in the now, even if you are uncomfortable, allows you to respond to the immediacies of your life in a measured way, keeping you in power of the situation and yourself.

Carlos had spent almost thirty years in the military, rising through the ranks to be a lieutenant colonel before retiring. His wife, Mika, had been a career military nurse. They had been married for twenty-four years when they came in at Mika's insistence. She said Carlos still acted like he was a military commander, becoming angry and "bossy" when life didn't move at the pace he expected.

"He's obnoxious at the bank, the grocery store, in restaurants … everywhere. If people don't 'hop to it,' as he says, he gets impatient, drums his fingers, scowls, looks around, and is generally obnoxious."

Carlos had been frowning through her litany. "Well, it's their job to be efficient. I don't see the problem. There is no excuse for dragging their feet. I'm sure their employer agrees."

Mika's face reflected her frustration. "Their job is not to ignore their other customers just to pay attention to you."

I suggested Carlos read Eckhart Tolle's *The Power of Now*, one of several excellent books about mindfulness. He came in a couple of sessions later. "I finished Tolle's book, and I can see why you suggested it. I've been living in the future and expecting things to go wrong, so I've been missing out on the present. Now I have to make some changes."

Carlos's military background helped him structure his transformation. He wasn't perfect, as he was quick to admit. "It's very hard to break the habit of being impatient, but I'm getting better," he observed several sessions later. "I've even told Mika she was right: I was obnoxious. And it's interesting how much better I'm being treated." I'm pretty certain the people dealing with Carlos hadn't changed their approach, but his management of his impatience let him see them differently.

We can all learn to live as much as possible in the present. Nobody will be perfect, and that's fine. The quest for perfection is a distraction from living in the moment. You want to be present, not perfect!

Mindfulness and meditation connect at the present. The peace you find in meditation helps support your search for presence, and staying in the present moment when you are meditating is critical. Balance in all things!

SILENCE YOUR INNER CRITIC

We all know that internal voice, the one making snide remarks and undermining our self-confidence and self-esteem, the voice telling us we're not good enough or smart enough or worthy enough to deserve happiness and achievement.

That voice has been there a long time and is very familiar, which is why it's so effective. Just when you think you're doing well or have accomplished a particular goal, the voice chimes in. "Right. You are kidding yourself if you think you will get that promotion. Why would they promote a loser like you?"

"Do you really think that good-looking person would be interested in talking to someone like you? Don't be ridiculous."

"Oh, what would make you think you looked even presentable in that outfit? It makes your hips look huge. And you look short. Ugh."

We, unfortunately, listen to that internal voice because it's familiar, which gives it much more power than it deserves. Rather than listening and agreeing, you need to confront the inner critic.

"Yes, I am going to get that promotion because I am strong and smart and a great worker."

"Yes, I believe that good-looking person will want to talk to me because I am interesting and smart and have good things to say."

"My hips are not who I am, and yes, I think I look great in this outfit."

We talked about affirmations earlier, and silencing your inner critic is a very useful application of their power. "I am powerful." "I deserve to be happy." "I am smart and strong." Those phrases combat the voice of the inner critic.

You have to be vigilant because that inner critic is "on" all the time. Don't let that little voice ruin your day or your life. Confront it immediately when it appears. It won't go away immediately, but as you use affirmations and confront the critic, you will begin feeling stronger and less likely to listen.

INNER CHILD

Dr. John Bradshaw focused on healing the inner child who exists in all of us, and I find his approach to resolving old issues by connecting with that part of yourself who is stuck at a particular age very effective with people who have been raised in a dysfunctional family. Being brought up by emotionally unavailable parents is a big factor in getting stuck. Often the inner child is the part of yourself empowering the inner critic.

In inner child work, you recognize the influence that your inner child or children has in how you react to situations. You seek to discover the age of the inner child by getting into a meditative state and looking inward. A "picture" of that inner you will emerge at some point. That picture may be a recollection of an actual photograph or a memory.

From that meditative state, you connect with that earlier version of yourself and engage in a dialog to discover what your inner child experienced or felt. Once you know the issue sticking your little self at that particular time of your life, you can then reconnect from your own adult perspective and help your inner child self move into the present.

I have an inner five-year-old. She got stuck when we moved to what became my hometown and our lives changed. My mom and I had been living with her mom while my dad traveled extensively for business. There were no kids in her neighborhood, so I had been around adults.

I had no idea how to act around people my own age, but suddenly we were in a neighborhood with lots of kids. I was overwhelmed, and my five-year-old self froze. After exploring my feelings with my therapist and meeting my inner five-year-old, over time I was able not only to help that inner child and me realize I was safe with people I didn't know but also to see the source of my lifelong discomfort with crowds and social situations. My inner five-year-old shows up every so often, and I can tell the days she's chosen my wardrobe since it tends toward primary colors, particularly red!

This summary of inner child work is a very brief synopsis of Dr. Bradshaw's comprehensive study. If you are interested in finding your inner child, I recommend his excellent *Homecoming: Reclaiming and Championing Your Inner Child.*

FINDING A THERAPIST

As with any relationship, finding a therapist who meshes with you requires some work.

There are external considerations and internal considerations to take into account with therapy. The external considerations include things like insurance coverage, deductibles, copays, covered number of sessions, location, and consistency of availability. Internal considerations are more subjective and include your comfort level with the therapist and his or her office, your sense of safety with the therapist, and your feelings about being able to confide in this person.

Insurance coverage can be complicated. Insurance companies contract with various providers, based on their own internal rules. Providers who have a contract with the insurance company are "in network," and what that means for you is, generally, the best financial arrangement.

Providers who are "out of network" mean you will be required by the insurance company to pay more out of pocket or may not be covered at all, depending upon your insurance contract. If finances are a consideration, you will want to call your insurance provider or go online to find out which therapists are in network and proceed from there.

The insurance *deductible* is the amount you must pay the therapist (and other medical providers) on your own before the insurance company pays anything. You pay the deductible to the therapist or physician directly. A growing trend in health insurance is called "catastrophic coverage," which is a policy for basically healthy people under which there is a very large deductible ($15,000 and up) that you must meet before they start paying. Many companies are trying to save money by providing insurance to employees at lower cost because of a large deductible. It's something to consider when you're choosing your annual plan through your employer.

The insurance *copay*, on the other hand, is the amount you must pay at each session. It is essentially your share of the cost of an office visit. The copay begins after the deductible is met and continues until you have reached the *out-of-pocket maximum*, which is the total of copays and other medical expenses you have to pay. Deductibles and prescriptions are not included. It's unusual for people to reach the out-of-pocket maximum unless they have had a really bad medical year, but if you do, the insurance company then covers 100 percent of all medical/therapy expenses.

Insurance contracts may also dictate the number of sessions you can have with a therapist per year. It's not unusual for the limit to be within the twenty-six- to forty-session range, but I have had clients whose benefit was limited to eight sessions a year. It's important to know those limitations when you first schedule with a therapist so that you can keep track. If you go over, the insurance company will refuse to pay, and you will be responsible to pay the therapist.

Some people choose not to use their insurance benefits for therapy because they would prefer their insurance company or their employer did not know they were accessing mental health benefits. This has been less a consideration at the time of this writing because of the prohibition for insurance companies to refuse coverage for preexisting conditions, but insurance company lobbyists are currently pushing hard to remove that prohibition.

Location is a consideration for convenience, but if you find a therapist you really click with, it's less of a factor.

Availability is important not only for a first appointment but for ongoing sessions. When you begin therapy or if your issue is acute, you may want weekly sessions and you want to be sure your therapist can accommodate your needs. Be prepared to be flexible with time as there are only so many late or lunch-hour appointments in a week. Some therapists offer Saturday schedules, but that's pretty unusual. My calendar is usually filled around lunch hours and later in the day with existing clients, so new people usually have to be willing to begin working with me in the mid-afternoon hours.

Some therapists are now using telemedicine as well as live meetings. I have several nonlocal clients with whom I meet via Skype or FaceTime or by phone. These electronic tools have expanded options for working with a therapist. There are a number of resources for finding therapists who may be outside your local area. If you search on the Internet for "psychologists" or "therapists," you will discover many of those sites. If you live in a sparsely populated or rural area where there are not therapists or you're not comfortable working with someone you're likely to see at the grocery store, telemedicine might be a good answer for you. Some insurance plans cover the costs of telemedicine, but you should check with them before you schedule with a remote therapist to be certain the company will cover it and the therapist is in-network.

The more subjective internal considerations are very important. You must feel comfortable with the therapist and in the office. It's critical to healing that you are in a space where you can relax. Fewer and fewer therapists have a traditional couch, as movies and TV would have you believe. My office has two comfortable leather easy chairs and a leather love seat. Clients choose where to sit at their first session and that often becomes their spot. I don't rearrange the furniture in my office because people are more comfortable and feel safer in familiar spaces.

Connecting with a therapist is kind of like a blind date, so you may not feel totally comfortable in the first session, but be alert to whether you like the therapist and his or her approach. Some therapists are very directive, and some are more organic and let things flow. You need to find the approach you believe will help you heal. You want to have someone who is able to figure out just how hard to push you so that you're uncomfortable but not freaked out. Some therapists reveal nothing of themselves and provide little feedback. Others are very interactive.

It's important to know a couple of things from a therapist's point of view. First, we want you to heal, and our feelings will not be hurt if, after a session or two, you decide we are not a match. It's part of the job. Not everyone will be a match.

Second, each of us has our specialties where we have the most training and feel the most able to help. When you are calling to set your appointment, tell the therapist what your issues are. Our job is to let you know if we have strength in that area, and if not, to refer you to a colleague we know who has that particular expertise.

Third, we only know what you tell us. We're not mindreaders. I believe what clients tell me is their truth. If you don't tell me your whole story or your true story, I'm not going to be effective as your therapist. You don't have to tell me or any therapist your whole story in the first or even the first ten sessions. Do recognize, however, that the less I know, the less help I am able to be.

Think of it this way: When you come into therapy you bring with you a box of puzzle pieces. We spend the first few sessions turning over the puzzle pieces and sorting them into however many puzzles are represented. Then we begin to assemble the puzzles. Sometimes pieces fit into more than one puzzle. Sometimes pieces don't fit anywhere but are important. Sometimes pieces surprise us by resolving a big issue when they seemed not to apply to anything. You know you're done with therapy when the puzzles are assembled and make sense.

Fourth, and perhaps most important, we don't judge. Whatever your choices have been they have been. If you are wanting to move past a choice you have made, we're there to help without judging. If you are feeling judged by your therapist, bring that up in session. It may be miscommunication between the two of you, or it may be time to change therapists.

Finally, give the relationship time. Remember, part of the process of therapy is to explore events in your life, and while it's nice to remember the good times, the reason you're there is to resolve the effects of the not-so-good or outright bad times. A lot of people get to the point where they're uncomfortable and quit. Stick it out. You'll be a happier person—eventually—if you do.

RESILIENT KIDS

Here's some good news. There are some people who grow up in the most odious and awful environments. They are abused in every possible way or neglected or objectified to the worst degree, and yet they grow up empowered and enabled. They are called *resilient kids*.

Somewhere along the way in their lives they have encountered someone who helped them see they are unique and wonderful human beings, deserving of love and support and caring. It may be a teacher or a neighbor or a babysitter or someone in their religious organization. It could be a grandparent or an aunt or uncle, or it might even be someone on television. Whatever the encounters, resilient kids got the message and rose above their particular life experience.

Being resilient means these people have drawn strength from adversity and used the lessons of their lives to their advantage. Resilient kids grow into resilient adults. Often they access support and therapy to work through the psychological effects of their traumatic childhoods and make sure they have put away what they need to store, but they don't dwell in the past and let it overwhelm them.

I firmly believe every victim has an inner survivor, an inner resilient kid who is there, ready to emerge and be strong. Together we can bring that inner resilient kid into the present and empower a resilient adult. Your life lessons have taught you survival skills. You might not recognize them as such, but in your work with this book and with your therapist, you can begin to discover those skills and put them to work in your daily life.

You are a strong survivor. The curveballs in your life have been powerful teachers. Now it's time to make them work for you. I believe in you. Join me.

Are You Emotionally Available?

It would not be unusual for the child of emotionally unavailable parents to be—*ahem*—emotionally unavailable. Since the root of psychology is really philosophy, we can ask a philosophical question: If I'm not connected to my emotions, how would I know I'm not connected to my emotions?

I have an answer. Take this quiz. Be honest—it won't be graded and you can't pass or fail. It's simply a tool to tell you where you might want to focus your healing efforts.

Rate yourself from 1 to 4 on each of the following questions.

1 = Never   2 = Sometimes   3 = Often   4 = Always

1. When I watch a movie, I really connect with the emotions of the characters.

    __ 1   __ 2   __ 3   __ 4

2. When people tell me they feel sad or scared or mad, I can share their emotion.

    __ 1   __ 2   __ 3   __ 4

3. When I look at a loved one, I feel many things at different times.

    __ 1   __ 2   __ 3   __ 4

4. I get over being mad quickly.

    __ 1   __ 2   __ 3   __ 4

5. I look forward to long relationships with friends and loved ones.

    __ 1   __ 2   __ 3   __ 4

6. When I hear a particular song related to events in my life, I have feelings I can identify.

    __ 1   __ 2   __ 3   __ 4

7. I like to laugh and to cry—to feel my feelings.

        __ 1   __ 2   __ 3   __ 4

8. I can figure out what other people are feeling based on their behavior.

        __ 1   __ 2   __ 3   __ 4

9. I am able to tell people what my emotions are.

        __ 1   __ 2   __ 3   __ 4

10. If I feel scared, I am able to work through it.

        __ 1   __ 2   __ 3   __ 4

11. No matter who I'm with, I am clear about who I am.

        __ 1   __ 2   __ 3   __ 4

12. I know my values and beliefs and I stick to them.

        __ 1   __ 2   __ 3   __ 4

13. I'm clear about my personal and relationship goals.

        __ 1   __ 2   __ 3   __ 4

14. I am able to talk about my feelings.

        __ 1   __ 2   __ 3   __ 4

15. I like to see emotions in others.

        __ 1   __ 2   __ 3   __ 4

Now add up your total score. If your score is:

1–15   Emotions are just a mysterious rumor to you, and you need to work hard to find your emotional self.

16–30   You have some connection with your emotional life, but you probably spend a lot of time in the Gray Zone.

31–45   You're connected emotionally in some areas of your life, but there are emotional experiences that motivate you to run and hide.

46–60   You're connected. You know yourself emotionally and are able to recognize and connect to emotions in others.

Now you know where you stand. The next step is to begin making some positive changes in the way you connect with other people. Your parents may have set your feet on a particular path, but that fact doesn't create a mandate for you to stay on that path. You get to choose. It's your life.

≈21≈

What Do Emotionally Available Parents Do?

You, unfortunately, found out in your childhood what emotionally unavailable parents do. In this chapter, we're going to explore what you can do to change your approach and be emotionally available for your own kids. And yourself!

BE THE PARENT

I am aware of how simplistic this sounds and how complex the reality is. Being a parent is a difficult balancing act in which the object on which you are currently balancing changes from moment to moment. At one stage in a child's life, it's important for you to be the one making the decisions and controlling the environment, and at another stage you have to be prepared to let them find their answers even if it means they might fail in the process. Parenting means being ready to be both a rescuer and a safety net.

Being the parent requires you to pay attention and be ready to respond—and sometimes react—to situations as they present. When your little people are infants and toddlers, you have to be ready all the time. As they grow, you need to be watchful but not necessarily always on the edge of your seat because you have taught your kids to make good decisions as they go along.

By the time they're teenagers you have to learn how to let go gradually, often despite your urge to hold on tighter. At that stage, you provide the safety net so that they don't fall all the way, but you need to let them make mistakes and learn so that by the time they're officially adults they have a foundation of skills and experiences to draw on to make good decisions.

Your kids don't need you to be their friend. That doesn't mean you have a distant relationship with them but rather they know you are there for them appropriately: not in competition with their friends but instead as a loving parent whom they can trust with their ideas and concerns.

You need to learn how not to look horrified when they tell you something you wish they had never told you, so the door is open for you to work on the issue or decision. They need to see you as fun and connected but in charge. It's how they will feel safe.

It's a tightrope stroll worthy of the Wallendas. If you stay in your emotions but not to the point you are overwhelmed by them, give your children guidance but not from the position of dictator, offer support without trying to take over, give them adventures while keeping them safe, and give them freedom without letting them run amok, then you're doing a great job on the high wire.

BOUNDARIES

Sometimes parents forget their children are separate individuals from them. After all, they've puked and pooped on you, counted on you for food and safety, learned how to walk and talk from you, and slept on and with you. You know every inch of their bodies.

As they grow, however, it's important they experience boundaries in both directions. You have to recognize their right to privacy, appropriate to their age, and they have to recognize your right to privacy. It's okay on both sides to show the respect of a knock before opening a closed door. That doesn't mean you don't enter their rooms, but instead you knock and announce yourself before you go in. You are demonstrating appropriate boundaries and perhaps heading off a kid intrusion on a private, adult moment in your life.

You also want your kids to understand the importance of boundaries in information they might share about your family with their friends or schoolmates—or, for that matter, with random strangers at Target. You can begin to teach the idea of private as soon as they have enough language to communicate. You could say, "This is about our family so it's private information. What that means is you don't share it with others."

You teach boundaries by demonstrating boundaries. Sometimes that means being careful about what you share around your little people. They are little sponges, absorbing the world around them and sometimes misinterpreting it. Be careful of things like gossip, off-color jokes, cussing, or opinions about others. The more vividly you present something, the more likely it is to stick in their brains. The first time little Jennifer busts out the F-bomb might be hilarious to you, but you need to not laugh and to tell her firmly that word is not okay. Otherwise you'll hear it again at the most inappropriate possible time. And invariably, if you've said something about your mother-in-law, it will be repeated when Grandma is present.

COMMUNICATION

Good communication with your kids is critical to emotionally available parenting. Using all the communication skills we've talked about throughout the book, including "I feel" language, reflective listening, the three-sentence rule, and clarity of language are all important, even with preverbal kids. Just as they learn to speak from listening to us, they also learn the good communication skills as you use them. Remember, kids understand language before they can speak clearly, and they will absorb the kind of language you use and how you use it.

When you want to communicate an idea to your little ones—or your teenagers, for that matter—be sure to look them in the eye and get their attention by saying their name. Don't lecture. Keep your language age appropriate. Be sure to listen to their answers, and be certain both of you are clear before you end the discussion. Then thank them for their time and attention. Good manners are part of good communication.

Don't yell. Yelling is a communication breakdown. It's very hard not to yell when your kids are totally ignoring you or openly defying you, but if you resort to yelling they will continue their behavior because, oddly, they can tune you out.

Quiet and direct is far more effective. You may need to put your hand on an arm or shoulder to be sure you have their attention, but keep your touch gentle and your voice low and soft. Meet their eyes directly. Outline the potential consequences. My brother, Jay, used to say, "You are approaching a spanking offense." He never actually spanked either of his kids because they knew he meant what he said.

STRUCTURE

Structure is creating a safe and predictable environment in which your kids know what to expect and when. Bedtime is best if it's always at the same time and has the same routine. Routine helps to solidify structure.

Structure makes kids feel safe. Everybody gathers for family meals. No phones or tablets at the table. Make your bed when you get up. Put your laundry away. No food in the bedroom. Good manners are expected. When kids know your rules and expectations from little personhood, it's easier to get them to stick to the rules, expectations, and structure when they are adolescents.

Yes, there are special times when they can stay up past their usual bedtime, for example, but they need to know it's a special exception and not a change in routine.

When you are clear about the structure in your life, it's easy for them to follow suit. Hence, you have to discipline yourself and be sure you live what you demand. You'll find it's a comfortable way to go about your day.

DISCIPLINE VS. PUNISHMENT

At its essence, discipline is teaching while punishment is humiliation. What humiliation teaches is powerlessness, and powerlessness leads to a lack of self-esteem.

Discipline *does not* involve hitting. It needs to be appropriate to the offense. Time-outs are effective with little people, and the formula of one minute per year of age is appropriate. You can make a time-out even more effective if you spend the time-out talking with your child about why they have a time-out and how to avoid it in the future. Once kids are beyond seven—depending upon the child and the level of maturity—time-outs are less effective.

Grounding is a poor solution as well because it also grounds the parents and it's hard to stick to for that reason. It also tends not to be offense specific. Instead, may I suggest *focused grounding*? This approach has the advantage of being offense specific in terms of timing and consequences. It's a pretty universal tool and effective for kids from four or five through the teen years.

Let's say that ten-year-old Felicia has been told no makeup until she's in seventh grade. Her older sister, Melissa, comes to you and says Felicia has been stealing her makeup and putting it on at school. When Felicia gets home, you sit down with her.

"Felicia, we've been very clear about makeup, and Melissa tells me you've been taking her makeup and putting it on at school. Those are two offenses against the family. For defying our policy, you'll have four hours of focused grounding. For stealing from your sister, you'll have another four hours. It will be convenient for me for you to be grounded on Saturday, starting at 1 PM."

During the focused grounding, Felicia has to accomplish tasks for the benefit of the family. She will have no access to any electronics—phone, TV, music—and computer only for homework. Tasks may include things like scrubbing grout, deep cleaning the bathroom, getting rid of the cobwebs in the basement, cleaning cupboards and kitchen drawers, grocery shopping and putting groceries away—anything outside normal chores. As parents, one or both of you will spend time with Felicia while she is accomplishing her tasks, talking about your family values and rules.

Punishment, on the other hand, is a version of revenge. It is often out of proportion to the offense and is usually delivered from a shaming position, as in, "You did this so you're a bad person." Punishment hurts self-esteem. Often punishment is physical, which only teaches a child that violence is acceptable and establishes fears and resentment. Discipline enhances structure and serves to unify parent and child.

PROBLEM SOLVING

Emotionally available parents are good problem solvers. They are careful not to let the problem run them, but rather they solve the problem at hand by staying in the Solver spot and using Solver skills. First, they define the problem, and remember, it's never a person. Then they brainstorm possible solutions, choose the most feasible response, get consensus, and solve the problem. This is very different from parents who intervene and attack on their children's behalf with teachers, coaches, neighbors, and friends. As tempting as it might be to jump in and fix a problem for your kid, what you are actually teaching them is powerlessness. Your message becomes "I don't trust you to solve this problem on your own with my support, so I'm going to take over." In psychological terms, this is called "learned helplessness," and it's exactly as it sounds.

When you teach your children problem-solving skills, you are teaching them not only to keep their personal power and see themselves as able and competent but also to manage frustration. People who know how to solve problems are far less likely to feel frustrated in human interactions because they have tools to conquer the issue at hand.

Start when they are little. Once Mason knows how to use his words to look for a solution, he is empowered to stay in that Solver spot. He will see himself as able and competent. Be there as his consultant and support, but let him figure it out. If he can't, nudge him gently in the right direction. Don't take over. Suggest, don't direct. You are helping Mason to feel in charge of situations, which creates a much stronger and more successful adult. It's a lifelong gift.

MANAGING DISAPPOINTMENT

Here's where I part company with the "everyone gets a trophy" philosophy. That approach does not teach the valuable skill of managing disappointment and leads to entitled adolescents and adults. We win and lose in life. You don't start your professional life as president of XYZ Buggywhip. You don't always get the job, promotion, life partner, or lottery win you want.

When we give every kid a trophy and don't keep score, we are predicting a world that doesn't exist in which children will fail because they are ill prepared to be gracious losers as well as gracious winners.

Remember, "no" is a complete sentence. It's very tempting to see the desired toy at Target as a special treat, but if you provide a special treat every time you go to Target, it becomes an expectation, which then becomes an entitlement. You may have to endure the embarrassment of a meltdown, but your kid will understand "special" means "special" and you're teaching about managing disappointment.

As with all skills, it takes practice. And patience on your part. If you can resist the temptation of special treats and show your firm boundaries, you are giving your children a great gift for real life.

DECISION MAKING

Along with problem solving, the process of making good decisions is a very important skill for children to develop. Once they are able to see themselves as able to make good choices, they will have better self-esteem and more confidence.

As with all these skills, they are best learned early. Start with either/or decisions, or what's called "forced choice." Chicken nuggets or mac and cheese? Red shirt or blue? As they get older and better at making those choices—and I fearlessly predict you will struggle through the terrible twos and snotty fours when they have no interest in either choice, so this will be a patience exercise for you—you can add a third option.

When they make their choice, affirm their choice and their skills. "Chicken nuggets it is. Good choice." As they get older, you want to ask them how they chose. Almost any answer is acceptable except, "I don't know." Nip that in the bud, or you will come to hate it when they turn into teenagers.

PATIENCE

I'm the perfect example of "I want patience and I want it right now." It's my biggest challenge to overcome, and I've battled it my whole life. I'm better, but I wish my family had been even more focused on teaching me.

When my brother, Jay, was about two and a half, he coined the term "to-now." He would fiercely glare at our mom and say, "I want a cookie to-now." That kind of sums both of us up.

Emotionally available people demonstrate patience, even if—like Jay and me—they have to fake it. I know our folks tried to overcome our impatience. One of their techniques was to ask us to make lists of pros and cons before making a decision. Another was, "Let's plan to talk about getting a puppy tomorrow." They managed that one for about six years before our beagle Honey joined our family.

Meditation enhances patience.

CRISIS MANAGEMENT

Your four-year-old takes a header off the picnic table onto the concrete patio, and there is blood everywhere as well as screaming, crying, and panic. If the screaming, crying, and panic are coming from you, that's not good crisis management. You need to be the island of calm in the middle of the chaos, even if you are terrified internally. Kids need to know their parents are in control even if the situation isn't.

Take a first-aid class, including CPR. It will give you a foundation of basic knowledge about how to respond to injuries of your kids. It will also give you confidence and a sense you can manage a situation.

Lindsay's six-year-old son, Cyrus, was sitting on the windowsill of his room, the window open behind him, watching his little brother, Ben, sort Legos. Ben threw a Lego at Cyrus, and he leaned back against the screen, which broke. Cyrus tumbled two stories onto the driveway. Lindsay had just completed a first-aid class and had told me she felt prepared if there was an emergency with the boys. She heard Cyrus scream and then silence, then Ben crying.

"I grabbed the phone and ran into Cy's room. Ben was sobbing and pointing out the window. I looked down and saw Cy lying still in the driveway and all my confidence immediately left. I was frozen for a minute, but then something inside took over. As I was running down the stairs, I dialed

911 and told them quickly what had happened. By the time I got to the driveway, I could see Cyrus stirring slightly. I knew from my class not to move him. His head was bleeding badly, but I remembered they said head injuries bleed a lot, so I knew to stay calm. Ben brought his blanket and gave it to me. 'For Cy,' he said, so I used it to protect him from the sun. The ambulance took Cyrus to Children's Hospital, and Ben and I rode along. Jeremy came there from work. Once he got there, I fell apart, but by then it was okay because Cy was in good hands and Ben had fallen asleep."

Cyrus had a skull fracture, but no permanent injury. Lindsay and Jeremy came to therapy for a while to work on their shared trauma. Jeremy repeatedly praised Lindsay for taking the first-aid class and staying so calm.

"Inside I wasn't calm at all but it was like something from the training kicked in and took over."

Even though Ben had witnessed the fall and the aftermath, both he and Cyrus came away from the experience without trauma because Lindsay had remained calm and in charge of the situation.

Being prepared in advance for emergencies is essential. While you're sorting laundry or making beds or making dinner or commuting, imagine what you would do if there were a fire or a tornado or an earthquake or a car accident or a medical emergency involving the kids. Discuss your ideas with your partner/spouse and make a firm plan together. Share the plan with the kids so that they know what to expect and what to do, and cross your fingers you never have to call on your plan.

You will not be perfect. You absolutely will make mistakes. Neither of those truths, however, predicts you will fail as a parent. There is a big gulf between mistakes made while trying your best and failing as a parent because you either don't try or don't care. When you make a mistake, own it, apologize, and correct it. The worst thing you can do is ignore it and make it again.

Being an emotionally available parent requires awareness. Pay attention to yourself and your kids: how you talk to and around one another, body language, wants and needs, boundaries, and the myriad of other subtle and critically important messages you share with one another.

Most of all, good parenting comes from love and kindness. When you start from those places, you will proceed to success.

Acknowledgments

While writing is truly a solitary endeavor, it is far from accomplished alone. To those whose lives are impacted by my "solitary" work, I offer my deepest gratitude.

To my truly amazing husband, Rod, whose love, patience, kindness, humor, silliness, insights, back rubs, laughter, and overall being excellent keep me sane and focused, thank you for thirty years of wonderful.

Thanks, also, to my dedicated agent Jennifer Weltz and the entire staff at the Jean Naggar Literary Agency, where I have been so spoiled since 1976. They are the embodiment of professionalism.

Gratitude also goes to Mali Moore, Sean Moore, Beth Chaplin, Stacey Weiner, and Brenda DeMotte who have all been kind enough to read and provide insights about this work in its early stages. I have become a better writer because of your observations.

Special thanks to the staff at HCI, particularly Allison Janse, editor extraordinaire.

I am grateful to those people who have been my teachers, intentional and inadvertent, throughout this life. Special thanks to my mentor and dear friend Judith Barnitt, whose wisdom and guidance have made me a much better person and therapist.

Thanks to my dear brother, Jay Christgau, and wonderful sister-in-law, Joan Christgau, who have been there even when I wasn't sure where "there" was. And to my parents, Ron and Ellen Christgau, who taught me to think and to laugh.

Finally, thank you to my clients who have trusted me to work with them on their puzzles over the almost thirty years I've been in practice. Your life threads of experience and courage have woven a strong fabric to support healing among your peers.

Bibliography

Reading resources in mental health healing can provide great auxiliary materials for working with a therapist and/or clarification or new thinking perspectives on various subjects. As with all lists, this bibliography is limited by timing. New works come out all the time and deserve your attention. The following list includes books currently available.

Arabi, Shahida. *Becoming the Narcissist's Nightmare: How to Devalue and Discard the Narcissist While Supplying Yourself.* SCW Archer Publishing, 2016.

Beattie, Melody. *Codependent No More: How to Stop Controlling Others and Start Caring for Yourself.* Hazelden Publishing, 2nd edition, 2010.

Bradshaw, John. *Homecoming: Reclaiming and Healing Your Inner Child.* Random House, reprint 2013.

Brown, Brené. *Braving the Wilderness: The Quest for True Belonging and the Courage to Stand Alone.* Random House, 2017.

Collins, Bryn. *Emotional Unavailability. Recognizing It, Understanding It, and Avoiding Its Trap.* McGraw Hill, 1997. (Shameless self-promotion)

Fjelstad, Margalis. *Stop Caretaking the Borderline or Narcissist: How to End the Drama and Get On with Life.* Rowman & Littlefield Publishers, 2013.

Forward, Susan, and Craig Buck. *Toxic Parents: Overcoming Their Hurtful Legacy and Reclaiming Your Life.* Random House, 2009.

Goleman, Daniel. *Emotional Intelligence. Why It Can Matter More Than IQ.* Random House/Bantam, 2012.

Goulston, Mark. *Talking to Crazy: How to Deal with the Irrational and Impossible People in Your Life.* AMACOM, 2015.

Kabat-Zinn, Jon. *Mindfulness for Beginners: Reclaiming the Present Moment—and Your Life*. Sounds True, 2012.

Katherine, Anne. *Boundaries Where You End and I Begin: How to Recognize and Set Healthy Boundaries*. Hazelden Publishing, 2010.

Kreisman, Jerold J., and Hal Strauss. *I Hate You—Don't Leave Me: Understanding the Borderline Personality*. TarcherPerigee, 2010.

Love, Troy L. *Finding Peace: A Workbook on Healing from Loss, Neglect, Rejection, Abandonment, Betrayal, and Abuse*. Amazon Digital Services, 2017.

Mason, Paul T., and Randi Kreger. *Stop Walking on Eggshells: Taking Your Life Back When Someone You Care About Has Borderline Personality Disorder*. New Harbinger Publishers, 2010.

McBride, Karyl. *Will I Ever Be Good Enough?: Healing the Daughters of Narcissistic Mothers*. Atria Books, 2008.

McLaren, Karla. *The Language of Emotions: What Your Feelings Are Trying to Tell You*. Amazon Digital Services LLC, 2010.

Melton, Glennon Doyle. *Love Warrior: A Memoir*. Flatiron Books, 2016.

Neuharth, Dan. *If You Had Controlling Parents: How to Make Peace with Your Past and Take Your Place in the World*. Harper Collins, 2009.

Pittman, Catherine M., and Elizabeth M. Karle. *Rewire Your Anxious Brain: How to Use the Neuroscience of Fear to End Anxiety, Panic, and Worry*. New Harbinger Publications, 2015.

Smith, Manuel J. *When I Say No, I Feel Guilty*. Bantam, 1985.

Stern, Robin. *The Gaslight Effect: How to Spot and Survive the Hidden Manipulation Others Use to Control Your Life*. Harmony, reprint edition 2007.

See also *esteemology.com*.

Index